CW01433115

JETHRO TULL 25TH

COMPLETE LYRICS

JETHRO TULL 25TH

COMPLETE LYRICS

Edited by
Karl Schramm and Gerard J. Burns

PALMYRA

Special thanks to:

Ian Anderson, Martin Barre, David Palmer, Mick Abrahams, Kenny Wylie, Gerd Burkhardt, David Rees, Bogdan Zarkowski, Alasdair George, Chrysalis Music London, Oliver Dallman / Chrysalis Music Köln, Friends Of Fairport, Windoc Film Peter Hägner, Holger Wedell, Hans A. Spoerle, Gerrit De Geus, Bert Maessen, Georg Stein, Kathrin Razum, Ohrwurm Musik, Peter Sauter, Jong Hi Schramm

Ian Anderson is donating all of his royalties in respect of this book to:
The Animal Health Trust, P.O. Box 5, Newmarket, Suffolk CB8 7DW, England.

All lyrics written by Ian Anderson except *Coronach* (David Palmer), *Sunshine Day*, *Move On Alone* (Mick Abrahams), and *The Story Of The Hare Who Lost His Spectacles* (Jeffrey Hammond).

A NEW DAY, the independent quarterly Jethro Tull information magazine.
Published by David Rees, 75 Wren Way, Hants GU14 8TA, England.

Editor's note: The book was produced in close cooperation with Ian Anderson. Some of the photographic material was provided by him, he also re-read and approved the lyrics. In the course of an extensive conversation held in May 1992 Ian Anderson gave a lot of information about the history and development of Jethro Tull and made in-depth comments on all of the band's LPs and some specific songs. The whole conversation has been condensed and is published as *Talking Tull*, in which the LP titles form the chronological framework. Ian Anderson's comments do not always refer directly to the respective LP, though; in some cases the LP title only sparked off a particular comment. In the interest of an authentic reproduction of the talks, the chronological order of the LPs as they appear in the book was adhered to.

Karl Schramm, born in 1956, lives and works as a musician and producer in Ludwigshafen, Germany. *Gerard J. Burns,* born in Liverpool in 1952, has been living in Ludwigshafen, Germany, since 1975.

Contents

TALKING TULL

Ian Anderson on
Jethro Tull

This Was

At the time when we were ready to record this album, we had a bunch of fairly standard blues-based songs which I or Mick Abrahams or both of us had written, plus instrumental pieces like *Cat's Squirrel* and *Serenade To A Cuckoo*, that featured Mick and me respectively. But I felt that this kind of music would not be indicative of what we were going to play in the future, that it was just a starting point for introducing Jethro Tull to the public. And so it seemed to me that, whatever that album was going to be about, it would be more of a historical document in terms of showing the origins of Jethro Tull. And so the title *This Was* was very deliberate, in the sense of wanting to create an identity for the album that would put it into that historical perspective, in the light of subsequent albums. That it would be »This was Jethro Tull« as they used to be when they played at the Marquee Club, when they began playing together as a band. It seemed like it was an interesting turnaround: rather than showing four little babies or four tiny children on the cover, to make it four really old men. And it's interesting that the following year, when we went to America for the first time, I remember some little girl in Los Angeles saying to me, »You are forty years old.« I said, »No, I'm not, I'm only twenty-two« – whatever I was at the time – and she couldn't believe this. She really thought that Jethro Tull, because of the album cover, and because of the way that we really looked, were old guys! And it's a true story that three or four years ago, when I was forty, I made a point of asking some twenty-year-old girl somewhere in America, »O.k., now how old do you think I am?« thinking, well, maybe she would say, »twenty-two, twenty-three« – but no, she said, »forty!« So I seem to have been the same all the way through. In people's minds we have always been this kind of band. Which is why, I think, Jethro Tull's fans are so varied. They're not just teenagers, they're not just old folks, they're not just boys in leather jackets. It's a very, very varied audience. It has always been really a great mixture of people. So looking back, albums like *This Was* and the subsequent album *Stand Up* say a lot about Jethro Tull's roots in blues, and about Jethro Tull's subsequent influences – classical music, jazz and folk music, ethnic or world music, whatever you want to call it, rock'n'roll. On *This Was* and *Stand Up* you've actually got a lot of Jethro Tull's identity.

Stand Up

Stand Up was the beginning of moving away from being in a blues band with Mick Abrahams, where he and I were both sort of equal forces. There were very bad problems between Mick Abrahams and Glenn Cornick, they didn't like each other. There were problems that arose in the band in terms of Mick's commitment. He didn't want to travel through other countries, and he gave us an ultimatum and said, »I will only play three nights a week!« The rest of us just found that impossible, we wanted to play every night, we wanted to be successful! So we found it impossible to continue with Mick under those circumstances, which put me in the situation of then having to write all the music and come up with new ideas.

So for me it was a chance to – not get away from blues – but to try and look for some other ideas. Therefore we experimented with exotic instruments, and so mandolins, balalaikas, whistles, saxophones, all kinds of things just started to creep in. Indeed, some of those things I use even now. I don't necessarily think that *Stand Up*, for example, is a great album, beautifully played with terrific songs on it. In many ways the songs are naive, simple, a little self-conscious in some ways. They're not by any means, I feel, my best songs, particularly lyrically. But it was a pretty good album by the standards of 1969, and at least it was interesting and pretty original. It didn't sound like everybody else. And there were a lot of bands back then who were all very special. Bands like Yes, Led Zeppelin, Nice and King Crimson had their very special identities, they were really different from each other. It was good to be part of that, but not part of a particular kind of music. All those bands were so different from each other, we were all very separate, a tremendous variety. And in America I guess there were a few bands that were important and different as well, like Zappa and Captain Beefheart, Grateful Dead, all that kind of stuff, with a lot of identity. More so than, I think, it's possible to have today.

Benefit

Benefit and *Stand Up* were both album titles suggested by Terry Ellis, who was our manager at the time. In both cases I didn't like the titles, but Terry really wanted to have some involvement in a creative sense. He was responsible for the album covers on *Stand Up* and *Benefit* as well. So *Benefit* went on, I suppose, from *Stand Up* in the sense of having heavy-riff rock'n'roll and a few more acoustic or gentle moments. In some ways, I think, perhaps it was a darker album – it didn't have the warmth, the humour, the lightness of *Stand Up*.

The title *Sossity* was a pun on the word »society«, but Martin Barre didn't know that. He thought *Sossity* was some girl's name. He actually had a boat which he called *Sossity*.

Afterwards, when I heard he'd named his boat this and beautifully painted the name on it, I said: »Martin, that was just a joke about society!« So he sold the boat! It sounded like it was a strange and very feminine childlike girl's name and it was amusing at the time, but it's not a lyric that I feel comfortable with now. I couldn't sing you that song.

All the songs fall into three categories lyrically. There are those that I'm happy to get up and sing, that I have an emotional reaction and feel honest about, and there are those that instantly I know I just cannot sing, in no way. It could be a song from twenty years ago, it could be a song from six months ago, but certain things I just know I'm not gonna be able to get up and do, because I don't feel right about them anymore. Some of those songs are amongst Jethro Tull's most popular songs, but I cannot get up and sing them. I've tried, I can't do it. I don't want to go on and do something which is dishonest, which it would be, if I went on there and smiled and sang those words as if they meant something. And if people enjoyed listening to that, they would be enjoying a theatrical performance – and a lie. I would much rather go on and sing a song that means something to me even if the audience don't like it, but luckily usually the audience will like it, at least a little. And then there are a very few songs – less than ten – that I can do sometimes, and if I'm in the mood I can be cheerful about them and it doesn't worry me too much that it's not a great song to sing. I'll give you an example: the song *Living In The Past*. As a piece of music I think it's quite a lot of fun, I still enjoy playing the thing, but I wouldn't want to sing all the words to it, 'cause I don't think it's very good. It sounds very »sixties« lyrically to me. *Aqualung* sounds »sixties«, but eighteen-sixty, nineteen-sixty, two thousand and sixty, that's o.k., that's a good lyric. *Farm On The Freeway*, to jump ahead twenty years, is gonna be fine in terms of lyrics. It's not tied into a certain place. So most of them I will either sing them or I won't sing them, and there's a few in between that maybe I'll sing if I'm in a good mood or I just feel like a little fun. So there are those few songs that occasionally become part of a concert, maybe for two or three weeks, and then they get pushed aside again; and then five years later they creep back in again for three weeks.

Aqualung

Aqualung is obviously seen by many people as being the seminal Jethro Tull album in many ways. They are right in the sense that it is the album that has continued to bring Jethro Tull to the attention of more people than any other. *Aqualung* was released at a time when Jethro Tull was just becoming popular in America and had already become popular in most European countries. So although it wasn't hugely successful in the year of its release it has continued to sell consistently since then.

Since I feel a little responsibility to the people who buy our records and who come to the concerts – I mean, I feel *a little* responsibility –, I'm interested to know what it is they like, how it is they have discovered Jethro Tull, what criticisms they might have. I'd like to find for these few years that I have yet to perform and make records – 'cause it will only be a few years – a good compromise between my tastes and the tastes of the people in the audience. I'm more interested in talking to the kids who are 16 to 25 than I am in talking to people that are in their late thirties or in their forties, because they – like it or not – are usually involved in seeing it with a nostalgic view, and I have a problem with nostalgia.

So it's not so easy for me to talk to the older fans about our music, because they are usually people who have followed Jethro Tull for many years. They have usually got ideas about music or concerts, things that are in their memories and are very personal for them. But they're not things that I can share with them. I wasn't there the night they met their wife or conceived their child. Maybe they think I was, because my record was playing on the stereo while they were busy on the floor. I don't feel that I should be responsible for this, that's their lives, not mine. But I am interested in what particularly younger audiences think, people coming for the first time to see Jethro Tull. It's a fresher and simpler view about it that I will usually hear from the younger ones, who maybe have discovered Jethro Tull because they heard *Aqualung*, or *Living In The Past*, or because they heard a track from the last album. It's just free of nostalgia, it's free of this sort of personal history, personal memories, it just has to do with now. But I only want to know a little bit, I don't want to know too much. Now the people who are becoming Jethro Tull fans are half of my age, or less than half of my age, in most cases they weren't born when we released the first albums. And so it's more difficult for me to understand what it is they see in the group. That's why I do sometimes talk to them – not every night, but maybe two or three times a week when I'm on tour. It's not market research, I'm not trying to decide the demographic reality of Jethro Tull, record sales or concert ticket sales, all I'm looking for is a little human contact, 'cause I like to know who it is I'm singing to.

I recognize a lot of the fans' faces, I've seen them at a lot of shows – maybe they wandered into a hotel bar, maybe they bought Dave Pegg a drink, and maybe I said »hello« and signed autographs or tour posters or programmes twenty times for them. I don't know their names, but I know their faces, I've probably spoken to them a few times, heard a comment about this and that. But they are probably people who've been with us for a long time. They're obviously a very important part of our audience. But they're not the only part, and I personally feel, during the few years left that we have as a band, it's important for me not just to be ignoring the people for whom Jethro Tull is truly exciting and new. And every night I play I have to keep in my mind that, for some people, this is the first time they see Jethro Tull, so it's the most important Jethro Tull concert they have ever been to. So for me, this isn't just going out on the stage saying, »O.k., it's you people again, hello, we're back,« for me it's really important to remember, somebody out there is going: »I never saw this before!« And I have to think about that when I play, because it's important that I don't waste this day, that I don't just make it another concert.

As I don't go out to rock concerts, I don't meet people, I don't have a lot of friends, I don't do any of the things that most people do, it is important for me to have contact with the audience, it's important for me to talk to people. It is important for me to talk about these things now and give a little extra information and a little bit of the reasons behind the things that I do and that I have done, particularly in regard to the more – I don't want to use the word intellectual, but the more cerebral side of it: the lyric writing in particular. I know that, to a lot of people, it's important what's in the lyrics, but it's different to every person who reads the lyrics or hears the song. They don't share my view of the world. They form their own picture, which is maybe a little bit different to mine, maybe very different to mine, it could be almost the same as mine. The important thing is: what they get from the lyrics is theirs, what the lyrics are for me is mine. Sometimes these two things are very close together and sometimes they're not. But it doesn't matter. That is why reading a piece of poetry, looking at a painting, listening to a piece of abstract music is a very special thing for the listener, for the observer, because you reach out and meet something.

You as a listener, a viewer, an observer, are also a creator, because the enjoyment from it is something that you put a piece of yourself into. So I think it's very important that, when people consider the lyrics, they mustn't be upset by the fact that I might say, »Well, this isn't really an important lyric,« because some may see three words in there that for them are very important about their lives and not just an accident – important to them, not important to me. So although I am the creator of my lyrics, I am not the creator of the way in which other people draw satisfaction from them or not. That's why the audience and the performer are so important together. What we always try to do when we go out onto a stage is to seek approval from an audience. But more than just looking for their applause, we're also looking for that little special something, that little bit of electricity, that little bit of evidence that you see in someone's eyes in the front row or in the second row, however far you can see, that says that what you're doing is actually creating a little spark somewhere which is the beginning, in a simple way, of some kind of an intellectual process as well as just an emotional one. Obviously the intellectual stuff, the real weightyness of the lyrics, is not that important, but it's a little bit important in the sense that it just makes that little spark, that little something that is an important part of the act of entertaining people.

There's got to be that little special something. It's a bit of magic, it's a bit of men together, clenched fists, leather jackets, spiky boots. It's a bit of a sexual thing with some pretty girl in the front row, sometimes it's even a bit of gay sex, in the sense that sometimes, particularly in English speaking countries, I will joke about homosexuality. And sometimes there will be somebody out there who is homosexual. For me it's an important thing to be able to make a joke and not offend them. And I hope that I can do that, and I hope that they allow me to do it!

There is this tentative, strange, dangerous relationship with the people who are the fans. A whole bunch of crazy people, and it's nice to know them, it's nice to know them a little bit. But it's not usually safe to know people too well. Not when they're fans, because it gets kind of mixed up with weird stuff. It's nice to meet people when you're on the stage, it's nice to sometimes meet some people when you're off the stage. To me a very nice thing about it is the fact that you get very close to people in some ways, but most of them you never meet. You're miles apart. Somehow you have this little way in which you do connect, just a precious strange moment on stage that is so mysterious. It's a very spiritual kind of a communion, and I'm not sure how it is for other performers. Is it the the same for Rod Stewart? Is it the same for Bono? I don't know. I'm not sure about other people in terms of their sincerity and how much they really care about the lives of the people that they do touch with their music. I hope that they are as concerned and worried about it as I have been for twenty-four years, because it scares the shit out of me that there are these people out there in the audience, and that we do have this mutual responsibility. It's a strange thing to be dealing with.

There was a time in my life when I got very upset with the audiences, back in around 1972, when we were performing *Thick As A Brick*. The difficulty then was trying to play the acoustic music that we didn't have to play when we were doing the heavy rock music of the *Aqualung* album. The audience was just about able to cope with the acoustic section in *Aqualung*, or in *Wind Up* or *My God*, knowing that they were going to get the big rock'n'roll riff any minute. With *Thick As A Brick* suddenly there was a lot more music that was really stretched out. The audiences, particularly in America, were not sympathetic to the concert atmosphere that it was necessary to maintain: that they had to be quiet in the quiet places, and could react and jump up and down in the loud bits. In 1992 in almost every country in the world the people have now learned how to respond to that song. I think people are less volatile now than they used to be at rock concerts. Probably less drugged as well, which also might help.

There were some crazy ideas on the *Aqualung* album, the sort of craziness of the song *Mother Goose*, a more surrealistic pastiche with summery motives, things in or around Hampstead Heath (a public park), strange characters, a little like nursery rhyme characters, but not about any one specific thing. It was just a place where I used to occasionally go and walk alone on Sundays when I first went to London and started playing; the biggest park near where I lived. And there were always all kinds of weird people there – still are. I was probably one of them at the time.

Cheap Day Return was based on a trip up to visit my father, who was in hospital at the time. In fact, *Cheap Day Return* and the song *Nursie* were both drawn from that. At that time I was away from home. I had not enjoyed a happy relationship with my father for some years of adolescence and although I guess around that time we were sort of patching it up, I was very aware that I might not see him again … I'm sure that for a lot of people at my age it's one of the things that you fear – or indeed, if it happens, it's a bad dream come true when you simply weren't there. Not that, on most occasions, there's anything you can do about it, but when you're thousands of miles away and somebody very close to you dies and you're just not able to be there – at that moment you feel very guilty, very much cut up and denied an opportunity to make your final farewell with somebody who is… Difficult emotions: entrusting my father's immediate life – or what remained of it – to nurses, medical staff, and hoping that they would take care of him until I got back from the next trip. The anticipation of that occured to me in fact on Preston platform, waiting for a train back down south. So all that was kind of a sad and slightly nervous moment. I think I wrote that on my way back on the train, but I do that a lot on trains.

The term »lush separation« in *Slipstream* could mistakenly be understood as a reference to alcohol, although it isn't. No alcohol references then or now, and certainly no references ever, as far as I'm aware, that have to do with drugs! I say that because on the album *Benefit* there was a line in *To Cry You A Song* that said »Flying so high…« – and would you believe it: it never occurred to me that this might be taken as a reference to drugs, but people back then thought that I was a serious druggie. And I don't think anybody believed me when I said that I didn't take drugs – I really didn't. And haven't. So to me it was like a really very naive and silly thing to have written, something that was actually an aeroplane song, singing about being away on tour or something, about some girl friend I had at the time. But how many people will have heard that and thought »Hey man, cool, peace«. So that's an example of very, very bad lyric-writing, because I created something which was almost bound to be misunderstood. And yet it just didn't occur to me what I was saying. I wasn't really that familiar with the vernacular of my contemporaries.

So I suppose I'm sympathetic to people like John Lennon saying *Lucy In The Sky With Diamonds* isn't a drug song – I still think it is. And most people probably still think that *To Cry You A Song* is a drug song, which I promise you it wasn't. So references to drugs and alcohol and that sort of things you probably won't find intentionally in any of the songs. At least not anything extolling their virtues or suggesting that I am drugged or drunk.

I think only a couple of times have I had too much alcohol, but it has been in the privacy of my own home. In fact, at times when I've been maybe working very late at night and I just haven't realised how long I haven't eaten, and I've just had a drink and come into the house and gone »Uh, oh, I don't feel well.« This happened to me twice actually in about the last ten years, and my wife found it extremely amusing as I was crawling up the stairs to the toilet to try and be sick.

The title track *Aqualung* has always been jointly credited as being written by Jennie Anderson, my first wife, and myself. We were – should I say – properly married for about a year. We separated and got divorced a couple of years later – not unhappily, it was just that we were both kind of young, she was Jewish and I wasn't. Socially, in the family sense and as to our religious background, we were very different people, and had we been ten years older everything would have been fine. But I think at that age it was very difficult, the pressure was enormous and the differences between us were very big, and we were both aware that I was becoming, if not rich, at least famous. She had been a secretary in the record company, and she obviously couldn't carry on working for a record company when we got married, because that would have been a little strange, not comfortable for anybody, the people in the record company especially. So she had to leave that job …

Becoming a housewife was probably as awful then as it would be now. I'm one of these really old-fashioned guys who believe that women should be jet-pilots, surgeons, teachers, engineers and things like that. I'm not a women's libber, but I always hated the idea – perhaps because of my own parental background – of ever having a wife who stayed at home and looked after the house, raised the children, cooked my dinner and had it waiting for me when I arrived home. That's always been a repulsive thought to me. I did want my first wife Jennie to do something that was not what I was doing. I didn't want her to be like Linda McCartney or Yoko Ono, not that those people, I think, existed at that time, in the public sense. But God … imagine having your wife on stage, playing a bloody tambourine, and the audience all hating it, saying, »Oh no, shit, he's brought his wife again!« So clearly I didn't want her to do that kind of stuff, and she wouldn't have wanted to do that either.

Jennie was interested in two things. One was photography, because her uncle had been quite a famous photographer in England, and she was interested in following that as a profession. Secondly she was interested in acting. I encouraged her to do these things, although it meant that even when I was at home, she would be out during the day, but she was doing something. Of course at the same time she was also meeting other people, and so she was forming a social life away from me. I didn't have any other friends or people other than the guys in the band, so we did begin to grow apart in that sense. After we split up she went on to be an actress. I remember seeing her on television thinking how really pleased I was that she'd at least made it to that point. At least we didn't hurt each other, no one got damaged.

One of the little episodes of that time was when she came back from some photographic assignment with some photographs of homeless people, tramps, down on the embankment next to the Thames in London. She had taken some photographs of this particular guy who was a very striking figure. He had a defiance and nobility about him, and indeed, so much better it would have been to have used her photograph with the guy's permission instead of that, I think, really not very attractive or well executed painting on the front cover of *Aqualung*. I've never liked the *Aqualung* album cover, although a lot of people think it's terrific. I didn't like the fact that it was made to look like me, or loosely look a little bit like me. Terry Ellis was wanting this to be a character: it could be like me, or it could be somebody else. And I said, »Hey look, this is really going to get dangerous, because there are bits of lyrical stuff in here that are alluding to the idea of God within man, the idea of purity, the godness within all people. But we don't want to start getting anybody thinking: ›Wait a minute, Ian Anderson is looking like this character of whom he says on the album cover something about God being within all men, even within *Aqualung*, or some reference like that. And it's meant to look like Ian Anderson, therefore Ian Anderson thinks he is God!‹« I said, »Terry, we're into dangerous stuff here, just make it look like some old guy!« But I got talked into this. I've always regretted letting it be that way.

Anyway, Jennie had scribbled down some lines about this guy. I said, »Hey, let's make this into a song.« We talked about the guy and she came up with a few lines, and I tried to show her how that could become a song. We wrote the lyrics to the first couple of verses and so she contributed to the lyrics of *Aqualung*. It's a good song, and it's probably the only time that I have ever written anything with anybody else lyrically.

Thick as a Brick / A Passion Play

Aqualung was seen by a lot of people to be a »concept-album«, which I didn't consider it to be. It was a collection of songs, four or five of them were related fairly strongly in terms of the subject material, talking about religion and whatever else. One side of the album focussed a little more, but not exclusively, on that religious theme, questioning the ideas of organized religion etc., but a bunch of songs on the record had absolutely nothing to do with anything else. When it came to doing *Thick As A Brick* it seemed important to try and come up with an album to follow *Aqualung,* which hadn't been hugely successful yet. So if *Aqualung* was a »concept-album«, where do we see this? The whole thing was really over the top. It wasn't done to make fun at our audience, it was done with a sense of fun that we wanted our audience to share with us. Lyrically it's o.k., but it's supposed to be done by this young boy, this precocious kid. And the whole album cover and everything about it was all done to make it pretty obvious that it was a joke. But of course, some people still thought that there was a Gerald Bostock who really did write all this, and even now people still ask me that! So it was done humorously, warmly, but it was meant to be a little bit of a satire about the whole idea of grand »rock-band-concept-albums«. However, it was a very successful album, and when it came to the next album I guess we all collectively fell into a trap of thinking, »Oh shit, maybe we should do this kind of thing again and instead of being silly about it, maybe we should take it seriously.« And I think that was a problem with *Passion Play* for me personally, looking back on it. It didn't have the humour or the warmth that *Thick As A Brick* did. Just as *Benefit* did not have that warmth and light-heartedness that *Stand Up* had. It doesn't mean that they're bad albums, it just means that there's some element missing that could have made them better.

Concerning the lyrics: »Really don't mind if you sit this one out« was a challenging statement to make to an audience in the sense of doing the whole song live, as we did on that year's touring. We walked on stage as a semi-famous band, I went to the microphone alone with an acoustic guitar, played a little introduction to people who were screaming and shouting, making all the noise, and opened with the words »Really don't mind if you sit this one out,« in other words: »Hey, if you want to ignore this or just fall asleep, that's up to you, we're going to do it anyway. ›My words but a whisper … ,‹ singing a quiet song, ›your deafness a shout … ,‹ but you're really not listening to me, you're just there for rock'n'roll or whatever.« And indeed, that is what happened, we did go on and play that album and it was murder, particularly in America. It got me to the point where I really just didn't want to do that anymore. That was the only time I ever felt like I didn't want to do any more concerts. It was difficult – and indeed, I suppose, a difficulty of our own making.

Let's remember: I think the reason the Beatles split up is because they never actually did any concerts where they could hear what they were playing, get any kind of musical satisfaction. And the more famous they became, the less chance they had to play live. Where was the music, the excitement of performance, to help them as a band through the problem periods that arose through the social and the marital differences and all the rest of it? I think if they had been able to go out and play decent shows, maybe they would at least have lasted a bit longer than they did. When they walked on stage, it was just non-stop screaming, people fainting or whatever, and that's just pointless. I mean, the Beatles had some great songs, and it's terrific when people scream and shout, but as soon as you start playing you want them to listen. Today, as soon as I start playing *Thick As A Brick* there's a great wave of recognition, but then immediately people go quiet. Except in Italy …

I think people are now a little less volatile and more tuned to the subtleties of old folks like us, who need more of a range of emotion in our performances. The audiences, too, are more receptive to an emotional range of intensity, a broader range of musical style. That's why we're still around and a lot of other people aren't, and why the people in our audiences are so different from each other, as opposed to being one social or demographic type. I suppose if you go and see Def Leppard or something, you're going to see a much more definable type of person in terms of clothing, in terms of age, in terms of behaviour. Just because our audience is so varied, can you imagine what it's like for me going up there and finding them, whether it's ten or twenty: somebody's first gig! They're at that age, fifteen or sixteen, when I know I became really keen on music, so I am really, really going to try hard, every night, to make it a gig they'll remember. The older folks should be very thankful that those younger kids are there, because that is one of the things that drives me on. I hope everybody else in the audience who is older can remember when it was their first gig. A lot of the time they do, they say, »Hey, I remember I first saw you in …« and I say, »O.k., fine, but tonight somebody else is also seeing us for the first time. So forgive me if I also pay them a little attention! This concert is not just for the old fans who have spent a thousand dollars on Jethro Tull tickets in the last twenty years, it is also for someone who has never been to a show and has no idea what's going to happen tonight.« I'm not just flattered because there's some younger kids there and they're coming to see us and maybe pretending to enjoy themselves. I'm genuinely curious to try and get from them the same reaction as I get from the rest of the audience, who are the old folks. It's a challenge that obviously gets harder as you get older.

Living In The Past

The original version of *Dharma For One* had this instrument in it called the »claghorn« that I'd invented. It was some primitive bamboo flute to which I'd taped a saxophone mouthpiece and an old bycicle horn, sawn off and fashioned on the end, so it made a kind of weird instrument. It was an attempt to come out with something that sounded really nasty, really strident and really horrid. And it did! It sounded amazingly awful. It was impossible to play in tune, you just went for it. This was one of these great things that were suddenly produced from a carrier bag on stage.

I think it is things like that which are part of the attraction of Jethro Tull for the Ramones, Iron Maiden or some of the heavy metal types, the punks and the trash metal types who admit to liking Jethro Tull. I think what it is they like about Jethro Tull is the sort of manic side, the aggression, the incredible something that fired them up.

When we played on some Swiss festival in 1991, we were doing our soundcheck and these strange guys came up at the end of it with Jethro Tull CDs and asked for our autographs. »Sure … « »This one is for Joey, but can you do this one for my mum, 'cause it's her birthday and she is really a big fan of yours,« and I wrote »To Joey's Mum« and said, »You guys are here on holiday? You're passing through or … « He said, »No, we're playing tonight.« I asked, »Oh, you're one of the bands?« They said, »Yeah, we're the Ramones.« I knew they were the punk band who'd more or less started it, they were the archetypal punk group in the U.S. before the Sex Pistols. So I made a point of coming down – we were towards the end of the concert and the Ramones were much earlier on. We'd come down from Turkey or Greece, don't remember, we'd been up all night. I dragged myself down after about two hours of sleep to catch a bit of the Ramones and I instantly thought, »Wow, this is just magic, I really would like to go on stage …« – 'cause they were just so good! Very simple, very basic, but it was going for it. I've bought two Ramones albums since then and I like them. I also like things like the Stranglers, although I didn't know too much about them at the time. But I've since bought some of their records and it's some great stuff of that period. Good songs with an attitude, with a sort of slightly chip on the shoulder, sort of persecuted, bad mood kind of attitude; a bit childish, a bit spoiled, not entirely pleasant, but good songs!

With people like the Ramones and some of the other punk bands there were very spirited and energetic performances, really basic, simple, aggressive rock'n'roll. I hope that in some ways some of Jethro Tull's music and performances have been half as good as the Ramones' or half as good as the Stranglers' in different ways. I think for a group of such broad musical tastes Jethro Tull does not compare badly with the best of the punk generation playing at that sort of level. Because when it's coming down to it, stuff like *Locomotive Breath*, or the loud bits of *Aqualung*, or whatever – I mean, I wouldn't say that I am Johnny Rotten, but what I'm putting forward is certainly not the stuff to win friends or take hostages. You're just aiming to kill when you do that stuff.

Whether you're John McEnroe and you've just lost the last point, or you're on stage doing that sort of a thing, you are like a time bomb. If somebody touches you, or somebody gets on the stage who shouldn't be there, or something happens, you really would kill at that moment! I wouldn't make a good bank manager for example, because I'd be exploding quietly twelve hours a day and probably would have died of a heart-attack or some evil cancer years ago. At least I think being lucky enough to get on a stage and explode in a controlled environment is a fortunate occupation to have!

I came back to England to live after having misguidedly, along with other members of the band, gone for tax reasons to spend a period of time in Switzerland. We never really became tax-exiles, because we always paid our taxes. After a year we were granted Swiss residency status, and the day our papers came through we all looked at each other and said, »Oh shit, let's go home!« Because the realisation we were really now Swiss residents suddenly just hit us. And I swear the next morning we were on the plane back to England! So we remained U.K. residents for tax purposes all the way through.

When I came back I found myself living alone in a rented mews cottage just off Baker Street. I think I was writing the *WarChild* album when I first moved to that particular Baker Street address, but I continued to live there at least into the period of writing the music for the next album. So the Baker Street references are really to do with my post-first-marriage life, living alone again and basically living out of a suitcase, as I then had got very used to doing. I didn't have too much in the way of trappings, things in my life. I didn't have a motor car, everything was simple.

The reference to »Edward Bear« in *Up The Pool* stems from this period. I think very possibly there was some thought in my mind – something about Edward Heath. Maybe it was because the Conservative Party had lost the election and that meant higher taxes; 83% under the new Labour government . Which really was too much! I like a simple world: my vote is for 50% taxes for us rich folks. For those of us who can afford to pay it I think we should pay half of our earned income in taxes. Once we've got to that upper income level, then a nice simple relationship – half for me, half for you. So I think by my standards, I should be paying more tax. I would go for a 50% tax rate if I was ruling our little country. But 83% was a mistake, was a great disincentive, and I think it was a tragedy at the time for my country to have, as it did, lost the affection, the industry and the input and the earning power of so many people in such a short space of time – and I don't mean Rod Stewart or anybody else, I'm talking about scientists, engineers. It took a long time for Britain to recover its position in terms of a meaningful economy.

WarChild

The name *WarChild* is taken from a Roy Harper song, it came up somewhere as a little passing reference, no more than that really. Probably the title song came first, or a few other bits and pieces on the album, things like *Skating Away ... ,* which had been recorded as one of the disastrous *Chateau Tapes* from a couple of years before, when we were trying to be tax-exiles. It was an album song collection totally unlike *Passion Play*. It was back to just a bunch of songs, some of them were light-hearted fun songs – a nice, good, accessible album. It had the *Bungle In The Jungle*-track on, which was a big hit in America as a single.

The song *SeaLion* is slightly ecological in content, probably influenced through being brought up in a place called Blackpool, where the sea was dirty grey, largely because of the dumping of all the town's sewage a very short distance off the shore. As an adolescent, a teenager, I used to go there when there was a big storm and the waves and great clouds of spray came crashing. We used to dodge the waves coming over the promenade there. Little did we know then that what we were dodging was every kind of variation of E coli bacteria known to man. The shit was flying when there was a storm at Blackpool, I tell you. I swear as the tide came in you would see lumps of faeces floating in the water, condoms and just every kind of filth imaginable. And children, little kids would be playing in the water! But no one ever did any water-tests back then. I grew up with that, and for that reason I have never in my life swum in the sea. I'm even reluctant to go in a swimming bath which some-body has been in during the last two or three years. Even now, if I go to some relatively nice beach wherever, I just don't want to go in there! I wander along the beach looking for the tell-tale signs of the septic tank outflows from the Caribbean hotel that I'm staying in, and then I tell my children: »Hey, don't go on to that beach, kids! I can see from that mark on the sand that that's where the discharge is.« So we all get our little phobias.

Minstrel In The Gallery

Again a slightly humourless, a slightly introvert album. It doesn't have that warmth in it which I think is important. Musically there is some pretty good stuff on it, but I think the band was suffering by the time of *Minstrel In The Gallery*. Jeffrey Hammond was a great guy, a great bass player, in the context of what he did, but he wasn't a real musician's musician. He just didn't know much about music. John Evans was really going off the boil. He had lost interest in rock music and was only playing Beethoven stuff endlessly on the piano. He was also drinking far too much. And he was not a healthy happy guy, having had a disastrous marriage and all the rest of it. A lot of things in the band were beginning to crumble. Barrie Barlow is a bit of a dissident type who was always picking fights and arguments, and the band, although it was playing reasonably well, just lacked real harmony.

We weren't really getting into it in the way that perhaps we were doing on *Thick As A Brick*. I think the last album that was made where the band did really click together again was the *Songs From The Wood* album, which – although we're jumping on a bit here – was an attempt to really try and get the thing to go as a band unit, with a social as well as musical identity. I deliberately would leave the studio and let them come up with some arrangements and ideas, it was better for me to leave them sometimes. But that shouldn't really be how it is – unfortunately it became the way of working, because it took my overbearing musical influence away and allowed them to contribute. That was, after all, quite a few years ago. I think we're all, even the guys who were in the band then and aren't now, a little more mature and grown up and more used to working with people! We have learned those social skills as well as musical skills, that we perhaps missed out on as itinerant rock musicians.

M.U. – The Best Of Jethro Tull

The title was Terry Ellis' contribution, Terry's idea of »Musicians' Union« as well. It stood for the idea of a union of past members of Jethro Tull, who were persuaded to get together to have a photograph taken; other than that it was just a compilation album.

Too Old To Rock'n'Roll: Too Young To Die

Too Old To Rock'n'Roll originally was an idea for a stage musical. I was in Switzerland, just on holiday over Christmas. I had worked on some ideas for songs, and when David Palmer came out we did another couple of weeks' work. Then the band joined us and we rehearsed and worked out some ideas, initially with a view to doing something different, something that would be a musical, theatrical sort of performance for somebody else. I can't remember if we had anybody in mind. It had some good songs on it. *Too Old To Rock'n' Roll* had the light, the humour and the warmth that wasn't there on the preceding album, and it's a slightly easier album to get into, to enjoy and to function within, although it's a bit quirky rock'n'roll. Stylistically it's not a very satisfying album for me, it's a bit too poprock, it doesn't have enough of the basic kind of blues or R & B type of thing for me.Things like *Taxi Grab* were o.k., first time for a long time that I played harmonica for example, things like *Salamander*, those were the nice bits of it.

Naturally enough I didn't draw the comic. In order to get some authenticity, I sketched out the story line and then we went to a guy who was a comic magazine writer. I can't remember what magazines he did, but he was someone reasonably well-known and we just said, »O.k., do what you do when you do a comic. Here's the story, but you make up the pictures, the blablabla, put it together,« and he did that.

Songs From The Wood

Obviously the more kind of English, folky music influence – with a small f, rather than a historical grand capital F of traditional, academic folk music, but a very small f for English folky music. After only ever living in hotels, or in the middle of London, or in other cities or town environments, I was, I think, the last member of the group to move out of town and go to live in the country. And when I went living in the country, I really went living in the country, not just in a leafy suburb or a village, but actually on a working farm. So suddenly what had been part of my childhood, spending a lot of time outdoors and being in more remote and rural places, was now a reality of day to day life. So that part of my life, having settled down again with my wife Shona and for the first time really owning a house and being in one place, had a stabilizing influence on my life. That gave me some definite place to put down some roots, and I think that gave the music a suitable anchoring point. But for me the important thing about the album is that it did bring together the guys in the band musically in terms of their involvement. Probably that was one of the albums – *Thick As A Brick* was one, *WarChild* to quite an extent too, *Passion Play* also from the band's point of view – in which the guys contributed with ideas and arrangements.

Heavy Horses

Heavy Horses obviously is the other sort of country, in the sense of rural, album that goes on from *Songs From The Wood*, but dare I say again, *Songs From The Wood* had the fun, the humour. Somehow again *Heavy Horses* is missing that kind of warmth.

I didn't really realize at that time how important the humour or the fun element was in Jethro Tull, which is why some of these albums lack maybe a little bit that element of levity – a lightness, a kind of »Let's not try to make every song a masterpiece, let's just play some songs that have no reason to be here other than they are amusing. They may not be startlingly original, they may not be terribly intricate or difficult to play, they're just fun to do.« Maybe it's because the mood in the band was responsible for that. A lot of the time there were frictions, difficulties within the group socially, that maybe meant that it wasn't as much fun as it should have been.

Stormwatch

Being at home again I was probably reading more newspapers, reading more magazines, watching current affairs and becoming more interested in things around me – even the weather, because of my involvements with farming and fish-farming. So I think some of the ideas for songs came from those sources. There is a foreboding about the album, there is a kind of slightly threatening feel to it, but it's not a bleak, cold record. Even things like *North Sea Oil* have got a bit of a bounce about them. They're not meant to be taken as serious political statements, they're just wry or cynical, but not negative or complaining, I hope!

A

A began as the idea of making a solo album outside Jethro Tull and the people that had been in Jethro Tull. Dave Pegg, who was in Jethro Tull as a bass player by then, after John Glascock's death, had never recorded with Jethro Tull, and so I felt it was o.k. to ask him to play on some songs that I was writing. I asked Eddie Jobson, who had been with a support band, the U.K., to play keyboards, and he brought his drummer Mark Craney with him. We didn't find a guitar player, so we asked Martin to join us on a couple of songs. It was the idea of just doing a couple of songs to see where it went. Anyway, we found that we worked very fast, very quickly together, perhaps it was the first time I had worked with an ostensibly different line-up of people altogether. So instead of recording just two or three songs we actually recorded about seven or eight in the period of a couple of weeks, and we went on to finish enough for an album.

Originally *A* was to stand for »Anderson«, not »Anarchy« as it was sometimes misunderstood, but indeed the album was far from rousing feelings of anarchic defiance. It was actually more often about the warning against such things. Lots of songs arose from things to do with current real-life scenarios, not so much about relationships, but more about things, about realities, about world-scale phenomena.

Black Sunday, one of the tracks on that album which I like best, is the one that was least well recorded. I think we had some loss of tape. It had to be savagely equalized when we were mixing. It doesn't sound a great song, but it was one that I really enjoyed. It was just a boy-girl song really, about the breaking up of a relationship. It was a much simpler, more direct lyric, although musically, and in terms of metre, it was a difficult song to sing: nowhere to take a breath!

The Broadsword And The Beast

This LP was distilled out of a lot of tracks that we recorded in '81 and '82, some of which eventually made it into the *20 Years Of Jethro Tull* compilation (*Jack-A-Lynn, Overhang, Too Many Too, Down At The End Of Your Road, I'm Your Gun, Mayhem, Maybe, Motoreyes, Rhythm In Gold, Jack Frost And The Hooded Crow*). A very popular album in Germany, possibly because of its symbolism. It is a good combination of heavy rock and folk elements plus some quite electronic stuff. I was playing keyboards on it. I wasn't a keyboard player, so my doing that job kept things from getting too crazy, kept things nice and fairly simple. Peter Vettese came in towards the latter part of that recording and did some of the tracks, but mostly the songs had come out of rehearsals where things were kept from getting too complicated. It was a chance for me to actually join in recording the backing tracks and be part of that process of recording, which made it more of a band feeling again, we were playing together live. A lot of the stuff was recorded in the studio pretty live with vocals which may or may not have been done again, but it was done very much as a group.

Walk Into Light / Under Wraps

Walk Into Light was the attempt to do the solo album that hadn't happened with *A*, but it was a collaboration really with Peter Vettese, rather than doing an album that was a predictable acoustic guitar and flute solo album. I thought it was a chance to look at some of the new technology, sequencers, samplers, high-tech synthesizers, that were becoming available, and to actually do something that would explore the possibilities of a different musical sound. It turned out with some good songs, but it sounds very early eighties-synthesizers. I would record those songs very differently if I were doing them now. But we went on, obviously, to do the *Under Wraps* album with the benefit of that bit of experience and made an album that I think was, although there are a couple of songs on it that I really don't like, a good example of techno rock. I did actually listen to nearly all of the album a few weeks ago and I was amazed how good it really was. I think it was a great album in terms of sound, in terms of the actual song, particularly I was singing really well. The best I've ever sung was on that record. Sadly it was the singing of that material on tour in '84 that actually caused the difficulties with my larynx. Whether it was the nature of the songs or just the intensity of it I don't know, but it was a shame. I can understand why a lot of Jethro Tull fans would be less satisfied with the sound of the album – it obviously does have a very electronic, more kind of techno sound to it –, but for me it's actually one of the albums that I find most pleasant to listen to. Certainly musically very competent, very well played, good stuff.

Crest Of A Knave

I didn't sing in '85, apart from one show that we did. I decided in '85 I wouldn't do anything musically at all and just concentrate on my fish farming activities. I wanted to expand that side of my business to get it much bigger as quickly as possible. I wanted it to be able to look after itself. So that involved a lot of my time for a short period and now involves very little of my time, since those ends were largely achieved a year behind schedule in 1991.

'86 we did a few concerts in Hungary and Israel and elsewhere. *Crest Of A Knave* came out of that period after we had done the summer tour in 1986. I remember writing the song *Budapest* in a hotel there, the morning after a show, about the vision of some slender and tall athletic creature who was serving sandwiches backstage. It was an easy lyric to write, ten minutes to scribble down half the lyrics for that one. I was having a cup of coffee, overlooking the not-so-blue Danube.

The title *Crest Of A Knave* came after the artwork. We worked on some of the images that were contained in the songs – you have more black cat references, since black cats are a favourite kind of animal for me. The major symbol thing was there, but we still didn't have a title for the album and the record company was going a bit panicky. *Crest Of A Knave* was just a not terribly clever pun on »crest of a wave«. But it just presented itself as an idea and people seemed to like it, so we went with it. It came out the same as *Catfish Rising*, the artwork was there first and the painting gave me the title.

20 Years Of Jethro Tull

We were just trying to come up with something that wasn't yet another *Best of …* album and the re-released or released material that had been hidden away before. Some stuff had to be finished recording, some of it just involved mixing, some of it was already mixed and just involved remastering.

Rock Island

I think *Rock Island* again missed out a little bit on having some of the humour elements there. It was there in an obvious fashion on things like *Kissing Willie* – which is not a great song, but it's a good fun song, and another one or two songs that were a bit more fun like that would have been good. *Rock Island* somehow had two or three songs too many that were just a little bit too serious.

Heavy Water – polluted rain – was based on one of my very first trips to New York. It was really, really hot and uncomfortable. Suddenly, blessed rain! I was standing out there getting wet and walking down the street, everybody else was busy running away from the rain. I realized that each drop of rain that had fallen on me had made a dirty black mark. It was raining coal and sulphur, very unpleasant.

Catfish Rising

There is a lot of acoustic-orientated material, which resulted from my writing songs particularly with mandolin, acoustic guitars and avoiding using keyboards. I had played keyboards on both of the previous albums; piano, organ, synthesizers were in there as part of the fabric. I just didn't have a keyboard in my studio at the time and found myself using more traditional stringed instruments, electric guitar as well. So it was an album born out of having fun making a kind of rock music using more traditional, woody sort of instruments and with an emphasis on blues as being the musical feeling behind most of it, rather than having classical or any folk references. A couple of songs in there are rather like »automatic-writing«-songs, a bit like *Mother Goose*, a little bit surrealistic – a sort of pastiche: images, things that dotted together. They don't necessarily tell a big story. They're just like lots of little ideas linked together, which maybe have a relationship and maybe don't. A couple of songs like that. A lot of lyrics in *Thinking Round Corners* were word associations, word-plays, little images, they're fun. For me fun both to sing and to write. Again for me that's an album that does have the humour, the warmth, a slightly careless feel about it which I like. But it doesn't necessarily mean that the next album will be the same way. I expect the next album will have certainly some more serious songs I've written already – maybe it is already headed on being more of a serious album, in which case I must try to learn from past experience to make sure I include three or four fun songs and don't make them all too serious.

THIS WAS

October 1968

My Sunday Feeling
Some Day The Sun Won't Shine For You
Beggar's Farm
Move On Alone (Mick Abrahams)
Serenade To A Cuckoo (Instrumental / Roland Kirk)
Dharma For One (Instrumental)
It's Breaking Me Up
Cat's Squirrel (Instrumental / Mick Abrahams)
A Song For Jeffrey
Round (Instrumental)

My Sunday Feeling

My Sunday feeling is coming on over me.
Now that the night is over
got to clear my head so I can see.
Till I get to put together
well that old feeling won't let me be.

Won't somebody tell me where I laid my head last night?
I really don't remember
but with one more cigarette, I think I might.
Till I get to put together
well that old feeling can't get me right.

Need some assistance. Have you listened to what I said?
Oh, I don't feel so good.
Need someone to help me to my bed.
Till I get to put together
that old feeling is in my head.

Some Day The Sun Won't Shine For You

In the morning – going to get my things together.
Packing up and I'm leaving this place.
I don't believe you'll cry, there'll be a smile upon your face.

I didn't think how much you'd hurt me.
That's something that I laugh about.
Bring in the good times, baby.
And let the bad times out.

That old sun keeps on shining.
But someday it won't shine for you.
In the morning I'll be leaving.
I'll leave your mother too.

Beggar's Farm

You're taking chances. And your reputation's going down.
Going out in the night-time. You think you make no sound.
But you don't fool me. 'Cos I know what you feel.
If you ignore the things I say –
someday soon's going to find you
'way down on Beggar's Farm.

I pay my money for no returns.
You think I need you. Going to find someone.
Oh, you don't fool me. 'Cos I know what you feel.
When you go out I won't ask you why.
And I won't worry when I see you lying
down on Beggar's Farm.

When you run to me, going to turn away.
Won't even listen when you try to say
that you were only fooling round –
'cos I know what you feel.
But if you ask me nicely, woman –
I'll wake up early one day soon and
I'll visit you down on Beggar's Farm.

Move On Alone
(Words and music by Mick Abrahams)

I feel so sad now that she's gone,
I've been loving that woman too long.
There is no place to go because my friends have all moved,
got nothing but sit in the sun.
Got tired of crying, guess I'll move on alone.

My bed is so empty and my heart is grown cold,
guess I'll just die before I grow old.
The place is untidy, that's 'cos I ain't done my dirt,
I've just grown tired of thinking.
Got tired of crying, guess I'll move on alone.

It's Breaking Me Up

So many long days. In so many ways.
I try to get through to what lies deep inside of you.
Oh, Baby. I said, you're breaking me up, woman.
Yeah, you're breaking me down.
You're lying in little pieces –
scattered all around.

You're doing your worst to see me get hurt.
You're waiting to see the tears running out of me.
But, oh, baby. I said you're breaking me up, woman.
You're breaking me down.
You're lying in little pieces –
scattered all around.

My tears have run dry and you wonder why.
I've found a new woman who don't do the things you can.
Oh, baby. I said you're breaking me up, woman.
You're breaking me down.
You're lying in little pieces –
scattered all around.

A Song For Jeffrey

Gonna lose my way tomorrow,
gonna give away my car.
I'd take you along with me,
but you would not go so far.
Don't see what I do not want to see,
you don't hear what I don't say.
Won't be what I don't want to be,
I continue in my way.

Don't see, see, see where I'm goin',
Don't see, see, see where I'm goin',
Don't see, see, see where I'm goin' to,
I don't want to.

Everyday I see the mornin' come on in the same old way.
I tell myself tomorrow brings me things I would not dream today.

STAND UP

September 1969

A New Day Yesterday
Jeffrey Goes To Leicester Square
Bourrée (Instrumental)
Back To The Family
Look Into The Sun
Nothing Is Easy
Fat Man
We Used To Know
Reasons For Waiting
For A Thousand Mothers

A New Day Yesterday

My first and last time with you
and we had some fun.
Went walking through the trees, yeah!
And then I kissed you once.
Oh I want to see you soon
but I wonder how.
It was a new day yesterday
but it's an old day now.

Spent a long time looking
for a game to play.
My luck should be so bad now
to turn out this way.
Oh I had to leave today
just when I thought I'd found you.
It was a new day yesterday
but it's an old day now.

Jeffrey Goes To Leicester Square

Bright city woman
walking down Leicester Square everyday.
Gonna get a piece of my mind.
You think you've not a piece of my kind.
Ev'rywhere the people looking.
Why don't you get up and sing?

Bright city woman
where did you learn all the things you say?
You listen to the newsman on TV.
You may fool yourself but you don't fool me.
I'll see you in another place, another time.
You may be someone's, but you won't be mine.

Back To The Family

My telephone wakes me in the morning –
have to get up to answer the call.
So I think I'll go back to the family
where no one can ring me at all.
Living this life has its problems
so I think that I'll give it a break.
Oh I'm going back to the family
'cos I've had about all I can take.

Master's in the counting house
counting all his money.
Sister's sitting by the mirror –
she thinks her hair looks funny.
And here am I thinking to myself
just wond'ring what things to do.

I think I enjoyed all my problems
where I did not get nothing for free.
Oh I'm going back to the family –
doing nothing is bothering me.
I'll get a train back to the city
that soft life is getting me down.
There's more fun away from the family
get some action when I pull into town.

Everything I do is wrong,
what the hell was I thinking?
Phone keeps ringing all day long
I got no time for thinking.
And everyday has the same old way
of giving me too much to do.

Look Into The Sun

To the sad song of one sweet evening
I smiled and quickly turned away.
It's not easy, singing sad songs
but still the easiest way I have to say.
So when you look into the sun
and see all the things we haven't done –
oh was it better then to run
than to spend the summer crying.
Now summer cannot come anyway.

I had waited for time to change her.
The only change that came was over me.
She pretended not to want love –
I hope she was only fooling me.
So when you look into the sun
look for the pleasures nearly won.
Oh was it better then to run
than to spend the summer singing.
And summer could have come in a day.

So if you hear my sad song singing
remember who and what you nearly had.
It's not easy singing sad songs
when you can sing the song to make me glad.
So when you look into the sun
and see the words you could have sung:
It's not too late, only begun,
we can still make summer.
Yes, summer always comes anyway.

So when you look into the sun
and see the words you could have sung:
It's not too late, only begun.
Look into the sun.

Nothing Is Easy

Nothing is easy.
Though time gets you worrying
my friend, it's o.k.
Just take your life easy
and stop all that hurrying,
be happy my way.

When tension starts mounting
and you've lost count
of the pennies you missed,
just try hard and see why they're not worrying me,
they're last on my list.
Nothing's easy.

Nothing is easy, you'll find
the squeeze won't turn out so bad.
Your fingers may freeze, worse things happen at sea,
there's good times to be had.
So if you're alone and you're down to the bone,
just give us a play.
You'll smile in a while and discover
that I'll get you happy my way –
nothing's easy.

Fat Man

Don't want to be a fat man,
people would think that I was
just good fun.
Would rather be a thin man,
I am so glad to go on being one.
Too much to carry around with you,
no chance of finding a woman who
will love you in the morning and all the night time too.

Don't want to be a fat man,
have not the patience to ignore all that.
Hate to admit to myself half of my problems
came from being fat.
Won't waste my time feeling sorry for him.
I see the other side through being thin.
Roll us both down the mountain
and I'm sure the fat man would win.

We Used To Know

Whenever I get to feel this way,
try to find new words to say,
I think about the bad old days
we used to know.

Nights of winter turn me cold –
fears of dying, getting old.
We ran the race and the race was won
by running slowly.

Could be soon we'll cease to sound,
slowly upstairs, faster down.
Then to revisit stony grounds,
we used to know.

Remembering mornings, shilling spent,
made no sense to leave the bed.
The bad old days they came and went
giving way to fruitful years.

Saving up the birds in hand
while in the bush the others land.
Take what we can before the man
says it's time to go.

Each to his own way I'll go mine.
Best of luck with what you find.
But for your own sake remember times
we used to know.

Reasons For Waiting

What a sight for my eyes
to see you in sleep.
Could it stop the sun rise
hearing you weep?
You're not seen, you're not heard
but I stand by my word.
Came a thousand miles
just to catch you while you're smiling.

What a day for laughter
and walking at night.
Me following after, your hand holding tight.
And the memory stays clear with the song that you hear.
If I can but make
the words awake the feeling.

What a reason for waiting
and dreaming of dreams.
So here's hoping you've faith in impossible schemes,
that are born in the sigh of the wind blowing by
while the dimming light brings the end to a night of loving.

For A Thousand Mothers

Did you hear mother –
saying I'm wrong but I know I'm right.
Did you hear father?
Calling my name into the night.
Saying I'll never be what I am now.
Telling me I'll never find what I've already found.
It was they who were wrong,
and for them here's a song.

Did you hear baby –
come back and tell you the things he's seen.
Did it surprise you
to be picked up at eight in a limousine?
Doing the things he's accustomed to do.
Which at one time it seemed like a dream
now it's true.
And unknowing
you made it all happen this way.

Did you hear mother –
saying I'm wrong but I know I'm right.
Did you hear father?
Calling my name into the night.
Saying I'll never be what I am now.
Telling me I'll never find what I've already found.
It was they who were wrong,
and for them here's a song.

BENEFIT

April 1970

With You There To Help Me
Nothing To Say
Alive And Well And Living In
Son
For Michael Collins, Jeffrey And Me
To Cry You A Song
A Time For Everything
Inside
Play In Time
Sossity: You're A Woman

With You There To Help Me

In days of peace –
sweet smelling summer nights
of wine and song;
dusty pavement burning feet.
Why am I crying, I want to know.
How can I smile and make it right?
For sixty days and eighty nights
and not give in and lose the fight.

I'm going back to the ones that I know,
with whom I can be what I want to be.
Just one week for the feeling to go –
and with you there to help me
then it probably will.

I won't go down
acting the same old play.
Give sixty days for just one night.
Don't think I'd make it: but then I might.

I'm going back to the ones that I know,
with whom I can be what I want to be.
Just one week for the feeling to go –
and with you there to help me
then it probably will.

Nothing To Say

Everyday there's someone asking
what is there to do?
Should I love or should I fight
is it all the same to you?
No I say I have the answer
proven to be true.
But if I were to share it with you,
you would stand to gain
and I to lose.
Oh I couldn't bear it
so I've got nothing to say.
Nothing to say.

Every morning pressure forming
all around my eyes.
Ceilings crash, the walls collapse,
broken by the lies
that your misfortune brought upon us
and I won't disguise them.
So don't ask me will I explain
I won't even begin to tell you why.
No, just because I have a name
well I've got nothing to say.
Nothing to say.

Climb a tower of freedom,
paint your own deceiving sign.
It's not my power
to criticize or to ask you to be blind
to your own pressing problem
and the hate you must unwind.
And ask of me no answer
there is none that I could give
you wouldn't find.
I went your way ten years ago
and I've got nothing to say.
Nothing to say.

Alive And Well And Living In

Nobody sees her here, her eyes are slowly closing.
If she should want some peace, she sits there, without moving,
and puts a pillow over the phone.
And if she feels like dancing no one will know it.
Giving herself a chance there's no need to show her how it should be.

She can't remember now when she was all in pieces.
She's quite content to sit there listening to what he says.
How he didn't like to be alone.
And if he feels like crying she's there to hear him.
No reason to complain and nothing to fear, they always will be …

Son

Oh I feel sympathy. Be grateful my son for what you get.
Expression and passion. Ten days for watching the sunset;
when I was your age amusement we made for ourselves.
»Permission to breathe sir,« don't talk like that, I'm your old man.
They'll soon be demobbed son, so join up as soon as you can.
You can't borrow that
'cos that's for the races and doesn't grow on trees.

I only feel what touches me
and feel in touching I can see
a better state to be in.
Who has the right
to question what I might do,
in feeling I should touch the real
and only things I feel.

It's advice and it's nice to know when you're best advised.
You've only turned thirty, so son, you'd better apologize.
And when you grow up, if you're good
we will buy you a bike.

44

For Michael Collins[1], Jeffrey And Me

Watery eyes of the last sighing seconds,
blue reflections mute and dim
beckon tearful child of wonder
to repentance of the sin.
And the blind and lusty lovers
of the great eternal lie
go on believing nothing
since something has to die.
And the ape's curiosity –
money power wins,
and the yellow soft mountains move under him.

I'm with you L.E.M.[2]
though it's a shame that it had to be you.
The mother ship is just a blip
from your trip made for two.
I'm with you boys, so please employ just a little extra care.
It's on my mind I'm left behind
when I should have been there.
Walking with you.

And the limp face hungry viewers
fight to fasten with their eyes
like the man hung from the trapeze –
whose fall will satisfy.
And congratulate each other
on their rare and wondrous deed
that their begrudged money bought
to sow the monkey's seed.
And the yellow soft mountains
they grow very still
witness as intrusion the humanoid thrill.

1 Michael Collins: astronaut, member of the Apollo 11-expedition; orbited the moon in mothership while
   Armstrong and Aldrin became the first men to walk on the moon
2 L.E.M.: lunar excursion module

To Cry You A Song

Flying so high, trying to remember
how many cigarettes did I bring along?
When I get down I'll jump in a taxi cab
driving through London town
to cry you a song.

It's been a long time –
still shaking my wings.
Well I'm a glad bird
I got changes to ring.

Closing my dream inside its paper-bag.
Thought I saw angels
but I could have been wrong.
Search in my case,
can't find what they're looking for.
Waving me through
to cry you a song.

It's been a long time –
still shaking my wings.
Well I'm a glad bird
I got changes to ring.

Lights in the street,
peeping through curtains drawn.
Rattling of safety chain taking too long.
The smile in your eyes was never so sweet before –
I came down from the skies
to cry you a song.

A Time For Everything

Once it seemed there would always be
a time for everything.
Ages passed I knew at last
my life had never been.
I'd been missing what time could bring.

Fifty years and I'm filled with tears and joys
I never cried.
Burn the wagon and chain the mule.
The past is all denied.
There's no time for everything.
No time for everything.

Inside

All the places I've been make it hard to begin
to enjoy life again on the inside,
but I mean to.
Take a walk around the block
and be glad that I've got me some time
to be in from the outside,
and inside with you.

I'm sitting in the corner feeling glad.
Got no money coming in but I can't be sad.
That was the best cup of coffee I ever had.
And I won't worry about a thing
because we've got it made,
here on the inside, outside so far away.

And we'll laugh and we'll sing
get someone to bring our friends here
for tea in the evening –
Old Jeffrey makes three.
Take a walk in the park,
does the wind in the dark
sound like music to you?
Well I'm thinking it does to me.

Can you cook, can you sew –
well I don't want to know.
That is not what you need on the inside,
to make the time go.

Counting lambs, counting sheep
we will fall into sleep
and we awake to a new day of living
and loving you so.

Play In Time

Got to take in what I can.
There is no time to do what must be done,
while I do some thinking.
Sleeping is hard to come by,
so we'll all sit down and try to play in time,
and we feel like singing.
Talking to people in my way.

Blues were my favourite colour,
till I looked around and found another song
that I felt like singing.
Trying so hard to reach you;
playing what must be played, what must be sung –
and it's what I'm singing.
Talking to people in my way.

Sossity: You're A Woman

Hello you straight-laced lady,
dressed in white but your shoes aren't clean.
Painted them up with polish
in the hope we can't see where you've been.
The smiling face that you've worn
to greet me rising at morning –
sent me out to work for my score.
Please me and say what it's for.
Give me the straight-laced promise
and not the pathetic lie.

Tie me down with your ribbons
and sulk when I ask you why.
Your Sunday paper voice cries
demanding truths I deny.
The bitter-sweet kiss you pretended
is offered, our affair mended.
Sossity: You're a woman.
Society: You're a woman.

All of the tears you're wasting
are for yourself and not for me.
It's sad to know you're aging
sadder still to admit I'm free.
Your immature physical toy has grown,
too young to enjoy at last your straight-laced agreement:
woman, you were too old for me.
Sossity: You're a woman.
Society: You're a woman.

AQUALUNG

April 1971

Side 1   Aqualung:

        Aqualung
        Cross-Eyed Mary
        Cheap Day Return
        Mother Goose
        Wond'ring Aloud
        Up To Me

Side 2   My God:

        My God
        Hymn 43
        Slipstream
        Locomotive Breath
        Wind Up

1. In the beginning Man created God;
and in the image of Man created he him.

2. And Man gave unto God a multitude of names,
that he might be Lord over all the earth
when it was suited to Man.

3. And on the seven millionth day
Man rested and did lean heavily on his God
and saw that it was good.

4. And Man formed Aqualung of the dust of the ground,
and a host of others likened unto his kind.

5. And these lesser men Man did cast into the void.
And some were burned; and some were put apart from their kind.

6. And Man became the God that he had created
and with his miracles did rule over all the earth.

7. But as these things did come to pass,
the Spirit that did cause Man to create his God
lived on within all Men: even within Aqualung.

8. And Man saw it not.

9. But for Christ's sake he'd better start looking.

Aqualung

Sitting on a park bench –
eying little girls with bad intent.
Snot running down his nose –
greasy fingers smearing shabby clothes.
Drying in the cold sun –
watching as the frilly panties run.
Feeling like a dead duck –
spitting out pieces of his broken luck.

Sun streaking cold –
an old man wandering lonely.
Taking time
the only way he knows.
Leg hurting bad,
as he bends to pick a dog-end –
he goes down to the bog
and warms his feet.

Feeling alone –
the army's up the road
salvation à la mode and
a cup of tea.
Aqualung my friend –
don't you start away uneasy
you poor old sod, you see, it's only me.
Do you still remember
December's foggy freeze –
when the ice that
clings on to your beard is
screaming agony.
And you snatch your rattling last breaths
with deep-sea-diver sounds,
and the flowers bloom like
madness in the spring.

Cross-Eyed Mary

Who would be a poor man, a beggarman, a thief –
if he had a rich man in his hand.
And who would steal the candy
from a laughing baby's mouth
if he could take it from the money man.
Cross-eyed Mary goes jumping in again.
She signs no contract
but she always plays the game.
She dines in Hampstead village
on expense accounted gruel,
and the jack-knife barber drops her off at school.
Laughing in the playground – gets no kicks from little boys:
would rather make it with a letching grey.
Or maybe her attention is drawn by Aqualung,
who watches through the railings as they play.
Cross-eyed Mary finds it hard to get along.
She's a poor man's rich girl
and she'll do it for a song.
She's a rich man stealer
but her favour's good and strong:
she's the Robin Hood of Highgate –
helps the poor man get along.

Cheap Day Return

On Preston platform
do your soft shoe shuffle dance.
Brush away the cigarette ash that's
falling down your pants.
And then you sadly wonder
does the nurse treat your old man
the way she should.
She made you tea,
asked for your autograph –
what a laugh.

Mother Goose

As I did walk by Hampstead Fair
I came upon Mother Goose – so I turned her loose –
she was screaming.
And a foreign student said to me –
was it really true there are elephants and lions too
in Piccadilly Circus?

Walked down by the bathing pond
to try and catch some sun.
Saw at least a hundred schoolgirls sobbing
into handkerchiefs as one.
I don't believe they knew
I was a schoolboy.

And a bearded lady said to me –
if you start your raving and your misbehaving –
you'll be sorry.
Then the chicken-fancier came to play –
with his long red beard (and his sister's weird:
She drives a lorry).

Laughed down by the putting green –
I popped 'em in their holes.
Four and twenty labourers were labouring –
digging up their gold.
I don't believe they knew
that I was Long John Silver.

Saw Johnny Scarecrow make his rounds
in his jet-black mac (which he won't give back) –
stole it from a snow man.

Wond'ring Aloud

Wond'ring aloud –
how we feel today.
Last night sipped the sunset –
my hand in her hair.
We are our own saviours
as we start both our hearts beating life
into each other.

Wond'ring aloud –
will the years treat us well.
As she floats in the kitchen,
I'm tasting the smell
of toast as the butter runs.
Then she comes, spilling crumbs on the bed
and I shake my head.
And it's only the giving
that makes you what you are.

Up To Me

Take you to the cinema
and leave you in a Wimpy Bar –
you tell me that we've gone too far –
come running up to me.
Make the scene at Cousin Jack's –
leave him to put the bottles back –
mends his glasses that I cracked –
well that's one up to me.
Buy a silver cloud to ride –
pack the tennis club inside –
trouser cuffs hung far too wide –
well it was up to me.
Tyres down on your bicycle –
your nose feels like an icicle –
the yellow fingered smoky girl
is looking up to me.
Well I'm a common working man
with a half of bitter – bread and jam
and if it pleases me I'll put one on you man –
when the copper fades away.
The rainy season comes to pass –
the day-glo pirate[1] sinks at last –
and if I laughed a bit too fast.
Well it was up to me.

1 Day-glo: dazzling orange colour; used, for example, for safety clothing on construction sites

My God

People – what have you done –
locked Him in His golden cage.
Made Him bend to your religion –
Him resurrected from the grave.
He is the god of nothing –
if that's all that you can see.
You are the god of everything –
He's inside you and me.
So lean upon Him gently
and don't call on Him to save you
from your social graces
and the sins you used to waive.
The bloody Church of England –
in chains of history –
requests your earthly presence at
the vicarage for tea.
And the graven image you-know-who –
with His plastic crucifix –
he's got him fixed –
confuses me as to who and where and why –
as to how he gets his kicks.
Confessing to the endless sin –
the endless whining sounds.
You'll be praying till next Thursday to
all the gods that you can count.

Hymn 43

Oh father high in heaven – smile down upon your son
who's busy with his money games – his women and his gun.
Oh Jesus save me!
And the unsung Western hero killed an Indian or three
and then he made his name in Hollywood
to set the white man free.
Oh Jesus save me!
If Jesus saves – well, He'd better save Himself
from the gory glory seekers who use His name in death.
Oh Jesus save me!
Well, I saw Him in the city and on the mountains of the moon –
His cross was rather bloody –
He could hardly roll His stone.
Oh Jesus save me.

Slipstream

Well the lush separation unfolds you –
and the products of wealth
push you along on the bow wave
of their spiritless undying selves.
And you press on God's waiter your last dime –
as he hands you the bill.
And you spin in the slipstream –
tideless – unreasoning –
paddle right out of the mess.

Locomotive Breath

In the shuffling madness
of the locomotive breath,
runs the all-time loser,
headlong to his death.
He feels the piston scraping –
steam breaking on his brow –
old Charlie stole the handle and
the train it won't stop going –
no way to slow down.
He sees his children jumping off
at the stations – one by one.
His woman and his best friend –
in bed and having fun.
He's crawling down the corridor
on his hands and knees –
old Charlie stole the handle and
the train it won't stop going –
no way to slow down.
He hears the silence howling –
catches angels as they fall.
And the all-time winner
has got him by the balls.
He picks up Gideons Bible –
open at page one –
God He stole the handle and
the train it won't stop going –
no way to slow down.

Wind Up

When I was young and they packed me off to school
and they taught me how not to play the game,
I didn't mind if they groomed me for success,
or if they said that I was just a fool.
So I left there in the morning
with their God tucked underneath my arm –
their half-assed smiles and the book of rules.
And I asked this God a question
and by way of firm reply,
He said – I'm not the kind you have to wind up on Sundays.
So to my old headmaster (and to anyone who cares):
before I'm through I'd like to say my prayers –
I don't believe you:
you had the whole damn thing all wrong –
He's not the kind you have to wind up on Sundays.
Well you can excommunicate me on my way to Sunday school
and have all the bishops harmonize these lines –
how do you dare to tell me that I'm my Father's son
when that was just an accident of Birth.
I'd rather look around me – compose a better song
'cos that's the honest measure of my worth.
In your pomp and all your glory you're a poorer man than me,
as you lick the boots of death born out of fear.
I don't believe you:
you had the whole damn thing all wrong –
He's not the kind you have to wind up on Sundays.

THICK AS A BRICK

April 1972

Thick As A Brick

Really don't mind if you sit this one out.

My words but a whisper – your deafness a SHOUT. I may make you feel but I can't make you think. Your sperm's in the gutter – your love's in the sink. So you ride yourselves over the fields and / you make all your animal deals and / your wise men don't know how it feels to be thick as a brick. And the sand-castle virtues are all swept away in / the tidal destruction / the moral melee. The elastic retreat rings the close of play as the last wave uncovers the newfangled way. But your new shoes are worn at the heels and / your suntan does rapidly peel and / your wise men don't know how it feels to be thick as a brick.

And the love that I feel is so far away: I'm a bad dream that I just had today – and you / shake your head and / say it's a shame.

Spin me back down the years and the days of my youth. Draw the lace and black curtains and shut out the whole truth. Spin me down the long ages: let them sing the song.

See there! A son is born – and we pronounce him fit to fight. There are black-heads on his shoulders, and he pees himself in the night. We'll / make a man of him / put him to a trade / teach him / to play Monopoly and / how to sing in the rain.

The Poet and the painter casting shadows on the water – as the sun plays on the infantry returning from the sea. The do-er and the thinker: no allowance for the other – as the failing light illuminates the mercenary's creed. The home fire burning: the kettle almost boiling – but the master of the house is far away. The horses stamping – their warm breath clouding in the sharp and frosty morning of the day. And the poet lifts his pen while the soldier sheathes his sword.

And the youngest of the family is moving with authority. Building castles by the sea, he dares the tardy tide to wash them all aside.

The cattle quietly grazing at the grass down by the river where the swelling mountain water moves onward to the sea: the builder of the castle renews the age-old purpose and contemplates the milking-girl whose offer is his need. The young men of the household have / all gone into service and / are not to be expected for a year. The innocent young master – thoughts moving ever faster – has formed the plan to change the man he seems. And the poet sheathes his pen while the soldier lifts his sword.

And the oldest of the family is moving with authority. Coming from across the sea, he challenges the son who puts him to the run.

What do you do when / the old man's gone – do you want to be him? And / your real self sings the song. Do you want to free him? No one to help you get up steam – and the whirlpool turns you 'way off-beam.

LATER

I've come down from the upper class to mend your rotten ways. My father was a man-of-power whom everyone obeyed. So come on all you criminals! I've got to put you straight just like I did with my old man – twenty years too late. Your bread and water's going cold. Your hair is short and neat. I'll judge you all and make damn sure that no-one judges me.

You curl your toes in fun as you smile at everyone – you meet the stares. You're unaware that your doings aren't done. And you laugh most ruthlessly as you tell us what not to be. But how are we supposed to see where we should run? I see you shuffle in the courtroom with / your rings upon your fingers and / your downy little sidies and / your silver-buckle shoes. Playing at the hard-case, you follow the example of the comic-paper idol who lets you bend the rules.

So!
Come on ye childhood heroes! Won't you rise up from the pages of your comic-books / your super crooks / and show us all the way. Well! Make your will and testament. Won't you? Join your local government. We'll have Superman for president / let Robin save the day.

You put your bet on number one and it comes up every time. The other kids have all backed down and they put you first in line. And so you finally ask yourself just how big you are – and you take your place in a wiser world of bigger motor cars. And you wonder who to call on.

So! Where the hell was Biggles when you needed him last Saturday? And where were all the sportsmen who always pulled you through? They're all resting down in Cornwall – writing up their memoirs for a paper-back edition of the Boy Scout Manual.

LATER

See there! A man is born – and we pronounce him fit for peace. There's a load lifted from his shoulders with the discovery of his disease. We'll / take the child from him / put it to the test / teach it / to be a wise man / how to fool the rest.

QUOTE

We will be geared to the average rather than the exceptional / God is an overwhelming re-sponsibility / we walked through the maternity ward and saw 218 babies wearing nylons / cats are on the upgrade / upgrade? Hipgrave[1]. Oh, Mac[2].

1 Hipgrave: schoolmate of Ian Anderson's and Jeffrey Hammond's
2 Mac: Jethro Tull's sound engineer at the time of *Thick As A Brick*

LATER

In the clear white circles of morning wonder, I take my place with the lord of the hills. And the blue-eyed soldiers stand slightly discoloured (in neat little rows) sporting canvas frills. With their jock-straps pinching, they slouch to attention, while queueing for sarnies at the office canteen. Saying – how's your granny and / good old Ernie: he coughed up a tenner on a premium bond win.

The legends (worded in the ancient tribal hymn) lie cradled in the seagull's call. And all the promises they made are ground beneath the sadist's fall. The poet and the wise man stand behind the gun, and signal for the crack of dawn. Light the sun.

Do you believe in the day? Do you? Believe in the day! The Dawn Creation of the kings has begun. Soft Venus (lonely maiden) brings the ageless one.
Do you believe in the day? The fading hero has returned to the night – and fully pregnant with the day, wise men endorse the poet's sight.
Do you believe in the day? Do you? Believe in the day!

Let me tell you the tales of your life of / your love and the cut of the knife / the tireless oppression / the wisdom instilled / the desire to kill or be killed. Let me sing of the losers who lie in the street as the last bus goes by. The pavements are empty: the gutters run red – while the fool toasts his god in the sky.

So come all ye young men who are building castles! Kindly state the time of the year and join your voices in a hellish chorus. Mark the precise nature of your fear. Let me help you to pick up your dead as the sins of the fathers are fed / with / the blood of the fools and / the thoughts of the wise and / from the pan under your bed. Let me make you a present of song as / the wise man breaks wind and is gone while / the fool with the hour-glass is cooking his goose and / the nursery rhyme winds along.

So! Come all ye young men who are building castles! Kindly state the time of the year and join your voices in a hellish chorus. Mark the precise nature of your fear. See! The summer lightning casts its bolts upon you and the hour of judgement draweth near. Would you be / the fool stood in his suit of armour or / the wiser man who rushes clear. So! Come on ye childhood heroes! Won't you rise up from the pages of your comic-books / your super-crooks and / show us all the way. Well! Make your will and testament. Won't you? Join your local government. We'll have Superman for president / let Robin save the day. So! Where the hell was Biggles when you needed him last Saturday? And where were all the sportsmen who always pulled you through? They're all resting down in Cornwall – writing up their memoirs for a paper-back edition of the Boy Scout Manual.

OF COURSE

So you ride yourselves over the fields and / you make all your animal deals and / your wise men don't know how it feels to be thick as a brick.

LIVING IN THE PAST

July 1972

Song For Jeffrey (*This Was*)
Love Story
A Christmas Song
Living In The Past
Driving Song
Bourrée (*Stand Up*)
Sweet Dream
Singing All Day
Witches Promise
Teacher
Inside (*Benefit*)
Just Trying To Be
By Kind Permission Of (Instrumental)
Dharma For One
Wond'ring Again
Locomotive Breath (*Aqualung*)
Life Is A Long Song
Up The Pool
Dr. Bogenbroom
For Later (Instrumental)
Nursie

Love Story

Going back in the morning time
to see if my love has changed her mind, yeah.
I know what I will find
that she is wasting time,
she could be picking roses.

Going back in the morning time
to see if my love has seen the light, yeah.
Oh, I told her last night
she could improve her sight,
she could be painting the roof.

Going back in the morning time
to see if my love has come around, yeah.
She offered me no sound,
her head is in the ground,
she could be calling for winter.

A Christmas Song

Once in Royal David's City stood a lonely cattle shed,
where a mother held her baby.
You'd do well to remember the things He later said.
When you're stuffing yourselves at the Christmas parties,
you'll just laugh when I tell you to take a running jump.
You're missing the point I'm sure does not need making
that Christmas spirit is not what you drink.

So how can you laugh when your own mother's hungry,
and how can you smile when the reasons for smiling are wrong?
And if I just messed up your thoughtless pleasures,
remember, if you wish, this is just a Christmas song.

Living In The Past

Happy and I'm smiling,
walk a mile to drink your water.
You know I'd love to love you
and above you there's no other.
We'll go walking out
while others shout of war's disaster.
Oh, we won't give in,
let's go living in the past.

Once I used to join in
every boy and girl was my friend.
Now there's revolution, but they don't know
what they're fighting.
Let us close our eyes;
outside their lives go on much faster.
Oh, we won't give in,
we'll keep living in the past.

Driving Song

Will they ever stop drivin' me?
Have they ever taken time to see
that I need some rest
if I'm to do my best?

Can I please stop workin' so hard?
They just tell me gotta close it hard.
Got to think of my health.
Can I be by myself?

Oh, they tell me I'll be home someday.
Well I doubt it if I continue this way,
'cause this hard life I've led
is making me dead.

Sweet Dream

You hear me calling in your sweet dream,
can't hear your daddy's warning cry.
You're going back to be all the things you want to be,
while in sweet dreams you softly sigh.

You hear my voice is calling
to be mine again,
live the rest of your life in a day.
Get out and get what you can
while your mummy's at home a-sleeping.
No time to understand
'cause they lost what they thought they were keeping.

No one can see us in your sweet dream,
don't hear you leave to start the car.
All wrapped up tightly in the coat you borrowed from me,
your place of resting is not far.

You hear my voice is calling
to be mine again,
live the rest of your life in a day.
Get out and get what you can
while your mummy's at home a-sleeping.
No time to understand
'cause they lost what they thought they were keeping.

Singing All Day

Singing all day, singing 'bout nothing.
Singing all day, singing 'bout nothing.
Singing all day, singing 'bout nothing,
oo, my, my, my,
oo, my, my, my.

Went down to the station to look for her there,
looked through the crowds for a glimpse of her hair,
nothing to see but the crowds keep a-staring at me,
my, my,
oo, my, my, my.

Down in the street, try'n' to remember,
shuffling my feet, outside a menswear,
is that her in the fur coat?
No it's not December yet,
my, my, my,
oo, my, my, my.

Singing all day, singing 'bout nothing.

Back to the house, maybe she'll phone me,
singing my song, feeling so lonely.
I'll sing very softly, so if the phone rings
I can hear it, I can hear it.

Singing all day, singing 'bout nothing.
Singing all day, singing 'bout nothing.
Singing all day, singing 'bout nothing,
oo, my, my, my,
oo, my, my, my.

Witches Promise

Lend me your ear while I call you a fool.
You were kissed by a witch one night in the wood,
and later insisted your feelings were true.
The witch's promise was coming,
believing he listened while laughing you flew.

Leaves falling, red, yellow, brown, all look the same,
and the love you had found lay outside in the rain.
Washed clean by the water but nursing its pain.
The witch's promise was coming, and you're looking
elsewhere for your own selfish gain.

Keep looking, keep looking for somewhere to be,
well, you're wasting your time, they're not stupid like he is.
Meanwhile leaves are still falling, you're too blind to see.

You won't find it easy now, it's only fair.
He was willing to give to you, you didn't care.
You're waiting for more but you've already had your share.
The witch's promise is turning, so don't you wait up
for him, he's going to be late.

Teacher

Well the dawn was coming,
heard him ringing on my bell.
He said, »My name's the teacher,
that is what I call myself.
And I have a lesson
that I must impart to you.
It's an old expression
but I must insist it's true.

Jump up, look around,
find yourself some fun,
no sense in sitting there hating everyone.
No man's an island and his castle isn't home,
the nest is full of nothing when the bird has flown.«

So I took a journey,
threw my world into the sea.
With me went the teacher
who found fun instead of me.

Hey man, what's the plan, what was that you said?
Sun-tanned, drink in hand, lying there in bed.
I try to socialize but I can't seem to find
what I was looking for, got something on my mind.

Then the teacher told me
it had been a lot of fun.
Thanked me for his ticket
and all that I had done.

Hey man, what's the plan, what was that you said?
Sun-tanned, drink in hand, lying there in bed.
I try to socialize but I can't seem to find
what I was looking for, got something on my mind.

Just Trying To Be

There was a time when you were so young and walked in their way.
They made you feel they loved you all-seeing they say.
You're going wrong if their game you don't play
and that the song I sing will lead you astray.

Unfeeling, feel lonely rejection,
unknowing, know you're going wrong.
And they can't see that we're just trying to be
and not what we seem,
and even now believe that it's not real and only a dream.

Dharma For One

Dharma[1], seek and you will find
truth within your mind, Dharma.

Dharma, each to his own we say,
together we'll end astray, Dharma.

Truth is like freedom, it doesn't fool me.
Being true to yourself, never think that you're free.
Dharma will come eventually.

1 Dharma: teaching of Buddha; universal law; insight into the meaning of reality

Wond'ring Again

There's the stillness of death on a deathly unliving sea,
and the motor car magical world long since ceased to be,
when the Eve-bitten apple returned to destroy the tree.

Incestuous ancestry's charabanc ride,
spawning new millions throws the world on its side.
Supporting their far-flung illusion, the national curse,
and those with no sandwiches please get off the bus.

The excrement bubbles,
the century's slime decays
and the brainwashing government lackeys
would have us say
it's under control and we'll soon be on our way
to a grand year for babies and quiz panel games
of the hot hungry millions you'll be sure to remain.

The natural resources are dwindling and no one grows old,
and those with no homes to go to, please dig yourself holes.

We wandered through quiet lands, felt the first breath of snow,
searched for the last pigeon, slate grey I've been told.
Stumbled on a daffodil which she crushed in the rush, heard it sigh,
and left it to die.
At once felt remorse and were touched by the loss of our own,
held its poor broken head in her hands,
dropped soft tears in the snow,
and it's only the taking that makes you what you are.

Wond'ring aloud will a son one day be born
to share in our infancy
in the child's path we've worn.
In the aging seclusion of this earth that our birth did surprise
we'll open his eyes.

Life Is A Long Song

When you're falling awake and you take stock of the new day,
and you hear your voice croak as you choke on what you need to say,
well, don't you fret, don't you fear,
I will give you good cheer.

Life's a long song.
Life's a long song.
Life's a long song.

If you wait then your plate I will fill.

As the verses unfold and your soul suffers the long day,
and the twelve o'clock gloom spins the room,
you struggle on your way.
Well, don't you sigh, don't you cry,
lick the dust from your eye.

Life's a long song.
Life's a long song.
Life's a long song.

We will meet in the sweet light of dawn.

As the Baker Street train spills your pain all over your new dress,
and the symphony sounds underground put you under duress,
well don't you squeal as the heel grinds you under the wheel.

Life's a long song.
Life's a long song.
Life's a long song.

But the tune ends too soon for us all.

Up The Pool

I'm going up the 'pool from down the smoke below
to taste my mum's jam *sarnies* and see our Aunty Flo.
The candyfloss salesman watches ladies in the sand
down for a freaky weekend in the hope that they'll be meeting
Mister Universe.

The iron tower smiles down upon the silver sea
and along the golden mile they'll be swigging mugs of tea.
The politicians there who've come to take the air
while posing for the daily press
will look around and blame the mess
on Edward Bear.

There'll be buckets, spades and bingo, cockles, mussels, rainy days,
seaweed and sand castles, icy waves.
Deck chairs, rubber dinghies, old vests, braces dangling down,
sun-tanned stranded starfish in a daze.

We're going up the 'pool from down the smoke below
to taste my mum's jam *sarnies* and see our Aunty Flo.
The candy floss salesman watches ladies in the sand
down for a freaky weekend in the hope that they'll be meeting
Mister Universe.

There'll be buckets, spades and bingo, cockles, mussels, rainy days,
seaweed and sand castles, icy waves.
Deck chairs, rubber dinghies, old vests, braces dangling down,
sun-tanned stranded starfish in a daze.

Oh Blackpool,
oh Blackpool.

Dr. Bogenbroom

I have one foot in the graveyard and the other on the bus,
and the passengers do trample each other in the rush.
And the chicken hearted lawman is throwing up his fill
to see the kindly doctor to pass the super pill.
Well, I'm going down, three cheers for Doctor Bogenbroom.
Well, I'm on my way, three cheers for Doctor Bogenbroom.

Well, I tried my best to love you all,
all you hypocrites and whores,
with your eyes on each other and the locks upon your doors.
Well you drowned me in the fountain of life and I hated you
for living while I was dying, we were all just passing through.
Well, I'm going down, three cheers for Doctor Bogenbroom.
Well, I'm on my way, three cheers for Doctor Bogenbroom.

Nursie

Tip-toes in silence 'round my bed
and quiets the raindrops overhead.
With her everlasting smile
she stills my fever for a while.
Oh, nursie dear,
I'm glad you're here
to brush away my pain.

A PASSION PLAY

July 1973

A Passion Play Part I & II

The Story Of The Hare Who Lost His Spectacles
(Jeffrey Hammond)

A Passion Play

»Do you still see me even here?«
(The silver cord lies on the ground.)
»And so I'm dead,« the young man said ----- over the hill
(not a wish away).
My friends (as one) all stand aligned although their taxis came
too late.
There was / a rush along the Fulham Road.
There was / a hush in the Passion Play.
Such a sense of glowing in the aftermath / ripe with rich attainments
all imagined / sad misdeeds in disarray / the sore thumb screams aloud,
echoing out of the passion play.
All the old familiar choruses come crowding in a different key:
melodies decaying in sweet dissonance.
There was a rush / along the Fulham Road / into the Ever-passion Play.
And who comes here to wish me well?
A sweetly-scented angel fell.
She laid her head upon my disbelief and bathed me with her ever-smile.
And with a howl across the sand I go escorted by a band of gentlemen
in leather bound ----- NO-ONE (but someone to be found).
All along the icy wastes there are faces smiling in the gloom.
Roll up, roll down.
Feeling unwound? ----- step into the viewing room.
The cameras were all around.
We've got you taped ----- you're in the play.
Here's your I.D.
(Ideal for identifying one and all.)
Invest your life in the memory bank ----- ours the interest and we
thank you.
The ice-cream lady wet her drawers, to see you in the passion play:
 take the prize for instant pleasure
 captain of the cricket team
 public speaking in all weathers
 a knighthood from a queen.
All of your best friends' telephones never cooled from the heat of your hand.
There's / a line in a front-page story / 13 horses that also-ran.
Climb in your old umbrella.
Does it have a nasty tear in the dome?
But / the rain only gets in sometimes and / the sun never leaves you alone.

Lover of the black and white ----- it's your first night.
The Passion Play / goes all the way / spoils your insight.
Tell me / how the baby's made / how the lady's laid / why the old
dog howls in sadness.
And your little sister's immaculate virginity wings away on the bony
shoulder of a young horse named George who stole surreptitiously
into her geography revision.
(The examining body examined her body.)
Actor of the low-high Q, let's hear your view.
Peek at the lines upon your sleeves since your memory won't do.
Tell me / how the baby's graded / why the lady's faded / why the old
dogs howl with madness.
All of this and some of that's the only way to skin the cat.
And now you've lost a skin or two ----- you're for us and we for you.
The dressing room is right behind.
We've got you taped ----- you're in the play.
Man of passion rise again, we won't cross you out ----- for we do love
you like a son ----- of that there's no doubt.
Tell us / is it you who is here for our good cheer?
Or / are we here / for the glory / for the story / for the gory satisfaction
of telling you how absolutely awful you really are.
There was / a rush along the Fulham Road.
There was / a hush in the Passion Play.

The Story Of The Hare Who Lost His Spectacles

(Written by Jeffrey Hammond)

This is the story of the hare who lost his spectacles.

Owl loved to rest quietly whilst no one was watching. Sitting on a fence one day, he was surprised when suddenly a kangaroo ran close by.

Now this may not seem strange, but when owl overheard Kangaroo whisper to no one in particular, »The hare has lost his spectacles,« well, he began to wonder.

Presently the moon appeared from behind a cloud and there, lying on the grass was hare. In the stream that flowed by the grass ----- a newt. And sitting astride a twig of a bush ---- a bee. Ostensibly motionless, the hare was trembling with excitement, for without his spectacles he appeared completely helpless. Where were his spectacles? Could someone have stolen them? Had he mislaid them? What was he to do?

Bee wanted to help, and thinking he had the answer began: »You probably ate them thinking they were a carrot.«

»No!« interrupted Owl, who was wise. »I have good eye-sight, insight and foresight. How could an intelligent hare make such a silly mistake?« But all the time Owl had been sitting on the fence, scowling!

Kangaroo were hopping mad at this sort of talk. She thought herself far superior in intelligence to the others. She was their leader; their guru. She had the answer: »Hare, you must go in search of the optician.«

But then she realised that Hare was completely helpless without his spectacles. And so, Kangaroo aloudly proclaimed, »I can't send Hare in search of anything!«

»You can guru, you can!« shouted Newt. »You can send him with Owl.« But Owl had gone to sleep. Newt knew too much to be stopped by so small a problem ----- »You can take him in your pouch.« But alas, Hare was much too big to fit into Kangaroo's pouch.

All this time, it had been quite plain to hare that the others knew nothing about his spectacles. And as for all their tempting ideas, well, Hare didn't care.

The lost spectacles were his own affair.

And after all, Hare *did* have a spare pair.

THE END

We sleep by the ever-bright hole in the door / eat in the corner / talk to the
floor ----- cheating the spiders who come to say »Please«,
(politely).
They bend at the knees.
Well, I'll go to the foot of our stairs.
Old gentlemen talk / of when they were young / of ladies
lost and erring sons.
Lace-covered dandies revel (with friends) pure as the truth -----
tied at both ends.
Well I'll go to the foot of our stairs.
Scented cathedral —— spire pointed down.
We pray for souls in Kentish Town.
A delicate hush ----- the gods / floating by / wishing us well -----
pie in the sky.
God of ages / Lord of Time ----- mine is the right to be wrong.
Well I'll go to the foot of our stairs.
Jack rabbit mister spawn a new breed of love hungry pilgrims
(no bodies to feed).
Show me a good man.
I'll show you the door.
The last hymn is sung and the devil cries »More.«
Well, I'm all for leaving and that being done, I've put in a request
to take up my turn in that forsaken paradise that calls itself »Hell« -----
where no-one has nothing and nothing is
well meaning fool, pick up thy bed and rise up from your gloom *smiling*.
Give me your hate and do as the loving heathen do.
Colours I've none ----- dark or light, red, white or blue.
Cold is my touch (freezing).
Summoned by name ----- I am the overseer over you.
Given this command to watch o'er our miserable sphere.
Fallen from grace / called on to bring sun or rain.
Occasional corn from my oversight grew.
Fell with mine angels from a far better place, offering services for
the saving of face.
Now you're here, you may as well admire all whom living has retired
from the benign reconciliation.
Legends were born surrounding mysterious lights seen in the sky
(flashing).
I just / lit a fag then / took my leave in the blink of an eye.
Passionate play ----- join round the maypole and dance (primitive
rite) (wrongly).

Summoned by name / I am the overseer / over you.
Flee the icy Lucifer.
Oh he's an awful fellow!
What a mistake!
I didn't take a feather from his pillow.
Here's the everlasting rub: neither am I good nor bad.
I'd give up my halo for a horn and the horn for the hat
I once had.
I'm only breathing.
There's life on my ceiling.
The flies there are sleeping quietly.
Twist my right arm in the dark.
I would give two or three for one of those days that never made
impressions on the old score.
I would gladly be a dog barking up the wrong tree.
Everyone's saved ----- we're in the grave.
See you there for afternoon tea.
Time for awaking ----- the tea lady's / making a brew-up and / baking
new bread.
Pick me up at half past none ----- there's / not a moment to lose. There
is / the train on which I came.
On the platform are my old shoes.
Station master rings his bell.
Whistles blow and flags wave.
A little of what you fancy does you good. (Or so it should.)
I thank everybody for making me welcome.
I'd stay but my wings have just dropped off.
Hail!
Son of kings / make the ever-dying sign / cross your fingers in the
sky for those about to BE.
There am I waiting along the sand.
Cast your sweet spell upon the land and the sea.
Magus Perde[1], take your hand from off the chain.
Loose a wish to still / the rain / the storm about to BE.
Here am I (voyager into life).
Tough are the soles that tread the knife's edge.
Break the circle / stretch the line / call upon the devil.
Bring / the gods / the gods' own fire.
In the conflict revel.

1 Magus Perde: medieval writer of passion plays

The passengers / upon the ferry crossing / waiting to be born / renew the pledge of life's long song / rise to the reveille horn.

Animals / queueing at the gate that stands upon the shore / breathe the ever-burning fire that guards the ever-door.

Man / son of man / buy the flame of ever-life (yours to breathe and breath the pain of living): living BE!

Here am I!

Roll the stone away from the dark into ever-day.

There was a rush / along the Fulham Road / into the Ever-passion Play.

WARCHILD

October 1974

WarChild
Queen And Country
Ladies
Back-Door Angels
SeaLion
Skating Away On The Thin Ice Of The New Day
Bungle In The Jungle
Only Solitaire
The Third Hoorah
Two Fingers

WarChild

I'll take you down to that bright city mile –
there to powder your sweet face and paint on a smile,
that will show all of the pleasures and none of the pain,
when you join my explosion
and play with my games.
WarChild dance the days, and dance the nights away.
No unconditional surrender: no armistice day –
each night I'll die in my contentment and lie in your grave.
While you bring me water and I give you wine –
let me dance in your tea-cup and you shall swim in mine.
WarChild dance the days, and dance the nights away.
Open your windows and I'll walk through your doors.
Let me live in your country – let me sleep by your shores.
WarChild dance the days, and dance the nights away.

Queen And Country

The wind is on the river and the tide has turned too late,
so we're sailing for another shore where some other ladies wait.
To throw us silken whispers: catch us by the anchor chains –
but we all laugh so politely and we sail on just the same.
For Queen and Country in the long dying day,
and it's been this way for five long years,
since we signed our souls away.
We bring back gold and ivory; rings of diamonds; strings of pearls –
make presents to the government
so they can have their social whirl
with Queen and Country in the long dying day.
And it's been this way for five long years,
since we signed our souls away.
They build schools and they build factories
with the spoils of battles won.
And we remain their pretty sailor boys –
hold our heads up to the gun
of Queen and Country in the long dying day.
And it's been this way for five long years,
since we signed our souls away.
To Queen and Country in the long dying day.
And it's been this way for five long years,
since we signed our souls away.

Ladies

Ladies of leisure, with their eyes on the back roads –
all looking for strangers, to whom they extend welcomes
With a smile and a glimpse of pink knees and elbows;
of satin and velvet – good ladies, good fortune.
Ladies.
They sing of their heroes: of solitary soldiers.
Invested in good health and manner most charming.
Whose favours are numbered (none the less well intended)
By hours in a minute; by those ladies who bless them.
Ladies.

Back-Door Angels

In and out the front door, ran twelve back-door angels.
Their hair was a golden-brown –
they didn't see me wink my eye.
'Tis said they put we men to sleep with just a whisper,
and touch the heads of dying dogs – and make them linger.
They carry their candles high – and they light the dark hours.
And sweep all the country clean with pressed and scented wild flowers.
They grow all their roses red and paint our skies blue –
drop one penny in every second bowl –
make half the beggars lose,
why do the faithful have such a will to believe in *something*?
And call it the name they choose,
having *chosen* nothing.
Think I'll sit down and invent some fool –
some Grand Court Jester.
And next time the die is cast, he'll throw a six or two.
In and out of the back-door, ran one front-door angel.
Her hair was a golden-brown –
she smiled and I think she winked her eye.

SeaLion

Over the mountains, and under the sky –
riding dirty grey horses, go you and I.
Mating with chance, copulating with mirth –
the sad-glad paymasters (for what it's worth).
The ice cream castles are refrigerated;
the super-marketeers are on parade.
There's a golden handshake hanging round your neck,
as you light your cigarette on the burning deck.
And you balance your world on the tip of your nose –
like a SeaLion with a ball, at the carnival.
You wear a shiny skin and a funny hat –
the Almighty Animal Trainer lets it go at that.
You bark ever-so-slightly at the Trainer's gun,
with your whiskers melting in the noon-day sun.
You flip and you flop under the Big White Top
where the long-legged ring-mistress starts and stops.
But you know, after all, the act is wearing thin –
as the crowd grows uneasy and the boos begin.
But you balance your world on the tip of your nose –
you're a SeaLion with a ball at the carnival.
Just a trace of pride upon our fixed grins –
for there is no business like the show we're in.
There is no reason, no rhyme, no right
to leave the circus 'til we've said good-night.
The same performance, in the same old way;
it's the same old story to this Passion Play.
So we'll shoot the moon, and hope to call the tune –
and make no pin cushion of this big balloon.
Look how we balance the world on the tips of our noses,
like SeaLions with a ball at the carnival.

Skating Away On The Thin Ice Of The New Day

Meanwhile back in the year One – when you belonged to no-one –
you didn't stand a chance son, if your pants were undone.
'Cause you were bred for humanity and sold to society –
one day you'll wake up in the Present Day –
a million generations removed from expectations
of being who you really want to be.

Skating away –
skating away –
skating away on the thin ice of the New Day.

So as you push off from the shore,
won't you turn your head once more – and make your peace with everyone?
For those who choose to stay,
will live just one more day –
to do the things they should have done.
And as you cross the wilderness, spinning in your emptiness:
you feel you have to pray.
Looking for a sign
that the Universal Mind (!) has written you into the Passion Play.

Skating away on the thin ice of the New Day.

And as you cross the circle line, the ice-wall creaks behind –
you're a rabbit on the run.
And the silver splinters fly in the corner of your eye –
shining in the setting sun.
Well, do you ever get the feeling that the story's
too damn real and in the present tense?
Or that everybody's on the stage, and it seems like
you're the only person sitting in the audience?

Skating away on the thin ice of the New Day.

Bungle In The Jungle

Walking through forests of palm tree apartments –
scoff at the monkeys who live in their dark tents
down by the waterhole – drunk every Friday –
eating their nuts – saving their raisins for Sunday.
Lions and tigers who wait in the shadows –
they're fast but they're lazy, and sleep in green meadows.

Let's bungle in the jungle – well, that's all right by me.
I'm a tiger when I want love,
but I'm a snake if we disagree.

Just say a word and the boys will be right there:
with claws at your back to send a chill through the night air.
Is it so frightening to have me at your shoulder?
Thunder and lightning couldn't be bolder.
I'll write on your tombstone, »I thank you for dinner.«
This game that we animals play is a winner.

The rivers are full of crocodile nasties
and He who made kittens put snakes in the grass.
He's a lover of life but a player of pawns –
yes, the King on His sunset lies waiting for dawn
to light up His Jungle
as play is resumed.
The monkeys seem willing to strike up the tune.

Only Solitaire

Brain-storming habit-forming battle-warning weary
winsome actor spewing spineless chilling lines –
the critics falling over to tell themselves he's boring
and really not an awful lot of fun.
Well who the hell can he be when he's never had V.D.,
and he doesn't even sit on toilet seats?
Court-jesting, never-resting – he must be very cunning
to assume an air of dignity
and bless us all with his oratory prowess,
his lame-brained antics and his jumping in the air.
And every night his act's the same
and so it must be all a game of chess he's playing –
»But you're wrong, Steve[1]: you see, it's only solitaire.«

The Third Hoorah

WarChild dance the days and nights away –
sweet child, how do you do today?
When your back's to the wall,
and your luck is your all,
then side with whoever you may.
Seek that which within lies waiting to begin
the fight of your life that is everyday.
Dance with the WarChild – Hoorah.

WarChild dance the days and nights away –
sweet child, how do you do today?
In the heart of your heart, there's the tiniest part
of an urge to live to the death –
with your sword on your hip and a cry on your lips
to strike life in the inner child's breast.
Dance with the WarChild – Hoorah.

WarChild dance the days and nights away –
sweet child, how do you do today?

1 Steve: reference to Steve Peacock, music critic

Two Fingers

I'll see you at the Weighing-In,
when your life sum-total's made
and you set your wealth in Godly deeds
against the sins you've laid.
And you place your final burden
on your hard-pressed next of kin:
Send the chamber pot back down the line
to be filled up again.

And the hard-headed miracle worker
who bathes his hands in blood,
will welcome you to the final *nod* –
and cover you with mud.
And he'll say, »You really should make the deal,«
as he offers round the hat.
»You'd better lick two fingers clean –
He'll thank you all for that.«
As you slip on the greasy platform,
and you land upon your back,
you make a wish and wipe your nose upon the railway track.
While the high-strung locomotive,
with furnace burning bright,
lumbers on – you wave goodbye –
and the sparks fade into night.

And as you join the Good Ship Earth,
and you mingle with the dust –
you'd better leave your underpants
with someone you can trust.
And when the Old Man with the telescope
cuts the final strand –
you'd better lick two fingers clean,
before you shake his hand.

MINSTREL IN THE GALLERY

September 1975

Minstrel In The Gallery
Cold Wind To Valhalla
Black Satin Dancer
Requiem
One White Duck/0^{10} = Nothing At All
Baker St. Muse
       Including:
       Pig-Me And The Whore
       Nice Little Tune
       Crash-Barrier Waltzer
       Mother England Reverie
Grace

Minstrel In The Gallery

The minstrel in the gallery looked down upon the
    smiling faces.
He met the gazes – observed the spaces between the
    old men's cackle.
He brewed a song of love and hatred – oblique
    suggestions – and he waited.
He polarized the pumpkin eaters – static-humming
    panel-beaters – freshly day-glow'd factory cheaters
    (salaried and collar-scrubbing).
He titillated men-of-action – belly warming, hands
    still rubbing on the parts they never mention.
He pacified the nappy-suffering, infant-bleating
    one-line jokers – T.V. documentary makers
    (overfed and undertakers).
Sunday paper backgammon players – family-scarred
    and women-haters.
Then he called the band down to the stage and he
    looked at all the friends he'd made.

The minstrel in the gallery looked down on the
    rabbit-run.
And he threw away his looking-glass – saw his face in
    everyone.

Cold Wind To Valhalla

And ride with us young bonnie lass –
    with the angels of the night.
Crack wind clatter – flash rein bite on an out-size
    unicorn.
Rough-shod winging sky blue flight on a cold wind
    to Valhalla.
And join with us please – Valkyrie maidens cry
    above the cold wind to Valhalla.
Break fast with the gods. Night angels serve
    with ice-bound majesty.
Frozen flaking fish raw nerve –
    in a cup of silver liquid fire.
Moon jet brave beam split ceiling swerve and light
    the old Valhalla.
Come join with us please – Valkyrie maidens cry
    above the cold wind to Valhalla.
The heroes rest upon the sighs of Thor's trusty
    hand maidens.
Midnight lonely whisper cries,
»We're getting a little short on heroes lately.«
Sword snap fright white pale goodbyes in the
    desolation of Valhalla.
And join with us please – Valkyrie maidens ride
    empty-handed on the cold wind to Valhalla.

Black Satin Dancer

Come, let me play with you, black satin dancer.
In all your giving, given is the answer.
Tearing life from limb and looking sweeter than the
    brightest flower in my garden.
Begging your pardon – shedding right unreason.
Over sensation fly the fleeting seasons.
Thin wind whispering on broken mandolin.
Bending the minutes – the hours ever turning on that
    old gold story of mercy.
Desperate breathing. Tongue nipple-teasing.
Your fast river flowing – your northern fire fed.
Come, black satin dancer, come softly to bed.

Requiem

Well, I saw a bird today – flying from a bush and the
    wind blew it away.
And the black-eyed mother sun scorched the butterfly
    at play – velvet veined.
I saw it burn.
With a wintry storm-blown sigh, a silver cloud blew
    right on by.
And, taking in the morning, I sang – O Requiem.
Well, my lady told me, »Stay.«
I looked aside and walked away along the Strand.
But I didn't say a word, as the train time-table blurred
    close behind the taxi stand.
Saw her face in the tear-drop black cab window.
Fading into the traffic; watched her go.
And taking in the morning, heard myself singing –
    O Requiem.
Here I go again.
It's the same old story.
Well, I saw a bird today – I looked aside and walked
    away along the Strand.

One White Duck/0^{10} = Nothing At All

There's a haze on the skyline, to wish me on my way.
And there's a note on the telephone – some roses on a
    tray.
And the motorway's stretching right out to us all,
    as I pull on my old wings – one white duck
    on your wall.
Isn't it just too damn real?
I'll catch a ride on your violin – strung upon your bow.
And I'll float on your melody – sing your chorus soft
    and low.
There's a picture-view postcard to say that I called.
You can see from the fireplace, one white duck
    on your wall.
Isn't it just too damn real?

So fly away Peter and fly away Paul – from the
    finger-tip ledge of contentment.
The long restless rustle of high-heeled boots calls.
And I'm probably bound to deceive you after all.

Something must be wrong with me and my brain –
    if I'm so patently unrewarding.
But my dreams are for dreaming and best left that
    way – and my zero to your power of ten equals
    nothing at all.

There's no double-lock defence: there's no chain on my door.
I'm available for consultation.
But remember your way in is also my way out, and
    love's four-letter word is no compensation.

I'm the Black Ace dog-handler: I'm a waiter on
    skates – so don't jump to your foreskin conclusion.
Because I'm up to my deaf ears in cold breakfast trays –
    to be cleared before I can dine on your sweet Sunday
    lunch confusion.

Baker Street Muse

Windy bus-stop. Click. Shop-window. Heel.
Shady gentlemen. Fly-button. Feel.
In the underpass, the blind man stands.
With cold flute hands.
Symphony match-seller, breath out of time.
You can call me on another line.

Indian restaurants that curry my brain.
Newspaper warriors changing the names they
     advertise from the station stand.
With cold print hands.
Symphony word-player, I'll be your headline.
If you catch me another time.

Didn't make her – with my Baker Street Ruse.
Couldn't shake her – with my Baker Street Bruise.
Like to take her – but I'm just a Baker Street Muse.

Ale-spew, puddle-brew – boys, throw it up clean.
Coke and Bacardi colours them green.
From the typing pool goes the mini-skirted princess
     with great finesse.
Fertile earth-mother, your burial mound is fifty feet
     down in the Baker Street underground. (What the hell!)
Walking down the gutter thinking,
     »How the hell am I today?« '
Well, I didn't really ask you but thanks all the same.

Pig-Me And the Whore

»Big bottled Fraulein, put your weight on me,« said the
     pig-me to the whore,
     desperate for more in his assault upon the mountain.
Little man, his youth a fountain.
Overdrafted and still counting.
Vernacular, verbose; an attempt in getting close to
     where he came from.
In the doorway of the stars, between Blandford Street
     and Mars.

Proposition, deal. Flying button feel. Testicle testing.
Wallet ever-bulging. Dressed to the left, divulging
   the wrinkles of the years.
Wedding-bell induced fears.
Shedding bell-end tears in the pocket of her resistance.
International assistance flowing generous and full
   to his never-ready tool.
Pulls his eyes over her wool.
And he shudders as he comes.
And my rudder slowly turns me into the Marylebone
   Road.

Crash-Barrier Waltzer

And here slip I – dragging one foot in the gutter –
   in the midnight echo of the shop that sells cheap
   radios.
And there sits she – no bed, no bread, no butter –
   on a double yellow line – where she can park anytime.
Old Lady Grey; crash-barrier waltzer –
   some only son's mother. Baker Street casualty.
Oh Mr. Policeman – blue shirt ballet master.
Feet in sticking plaster –
   move the old lady on.
Strange pas-de-deux –
   his Romeo to her Juliet.
Her sleeping draught, his poisoned regret.
No drunken bums allowed to sleep here in the
   crowded emptiness.
Oh officer, let me send her to a cheap hotel –
   I'll pay the bill and make her well – like hell you
   bloody will!
No do-good overkill. We must teach them
   to be still more independent.

Mother England Reverie

I have no time for Time Magazine or Rolling Stone.
I have no wish for wishing wells or wishing bones.
I have no house in the country I have no motor car.
And if you think I'm joking, then I'm just a one-line
   joker in a public bar.

And it seems there's no-body left for tennis: and I'm
    a one-band-man.
And I want no Top Twenty funeral or a hundred grand.

There was a little boy stood on a burning log,
    rubbing his hands with glee. He said »Oh Mother England,
    did you light my smile: or did you light
    this fire under me?
One day I'll be a minstrel in the gallery.
And paint you a picture of the queen.
And if sometimes I sing to a cynical degree –
    it's just the nonsense that it seems.«

So I drift down through the Baker Street valley,
    in my steep-sided un-reality.
And when all is said and all is done – I couldn't wish
    for a better one.
It's a real-life ripe dead certainty –
    that I'm just a Baker Street muse.

Talking to the gutter-stinking, winking in the same
    old way.
I tried to catch my eye but I looked the other way.

Indian restaurants that curry my brain –
    newspaper warriors changing the names they
    advertise from the station stand.
Circumcised with cold print hands.

Windy bus-stop. Click. Shop-window. Heel.
Shady gentlemen. Fly-button. Feel.
In the underpass, the blind man stands.
With cold flute hands.
Symphony match-seller, breath out of time –
    you can call me on another line.

Didn't make her – with my Baker Street Ruse.
Couldn't shake her – with my Baker Street Bruise.
Like to take her – but I'm just a Baker Street Muse.

(I can't get out!)

Grace

Hello sun.
Hello bird.
Hello my lady.
Hello breakfast. May I
    buy you again tomorrow?

M.U. – THE BEST OF JETHRO TULL

January 1976

Teacher (*Living In The Past*)
Aqualung (*Aqualung*)
Thick As A Brick (*Thick As A Brick*)
Bungle In The Jungle (*War Child*)
Locomotive Breath (*Aqualung*)
Fat Man (*Stand Up*)
Living in The Past (*Living In The Past*)
A Passion Play (*A Passion Play*)
Skating Away (On The Thin Ice Of The New Day) (*War Child*)
Rainbow Blues
Nothing Is Easy (*Stand Up*)

Rainbow Blues

Through northern lights on back streets –
I told the coachman, »Just drive me on.
It's the same old destination
but a different world to sing upon.«
So he threw back his head and he counted.
I jumped out about five to nine.
And I waved at the stage door-keeper –
said, »Mister, get me to the stage on time.«

Oh, but the rain wasn't made of water
and the snow didn't have a place in the sun
so I slipped behind a rainbow
and waited till the show had done.

I packed my ammunition.
Inside the crowd was shouting, »Encore«,
But I had a most funny feeling –
it wasn't me they were shouting for.
So when the tall dark lady smiled at me
I said, »Oh, baby let us go for a ride.«
And we came upon two drinks or four
and popped them oh so neatly inside.

Oh, but the rain wasn't made of water
and the snow didn't have a place in the sun
so we slipped behind a rainbow
and lay there until we had done.

Let me pack you deep in my suitcase.
Oh, there's sure to be room for two –
or you can drive me to the airplane
but don't let me catch those rainbow blues.

TOO OLD TO ROCK'N'ROLL: TOO YOUNG TO DIE

May 1976

Quizz Kid
Crazed Institution
Salamander
Taxi Grab
From A Deadbeat To An Old Greaser
Bad-Eyed And Loveless
Big Dipper
Too Old To Rock'n'Roll: Too Young To Die
Pied Piper
The Chequered Flag (Dead Or Alive)

Quizz Kid

Cut along the dotted line – slip in and seal the flap.
Postal competition crazy, though you wear the dunce's cap.
Win a fortnight in Ibiza – line up for the big hand-out.
You'll never know unless you try – what winning's all about –
be a quizz kid.
Be a whizz kid.

Six days later there's a rush telegram.
Drop everything and telephone this number if you can.
It's a free trip down to London for a weekend of high life.
They'll wine you; dine you; undermine you –
better not bring the wife –
be a quizz kid.
Be a whizz kid.

It's a try out for a quizz show that millions watch each week.
Following the fate and fortunes of contestants as they speak.
Answerable to everyone; responsible to all: publicly dissected –
brain cells spattered on the walls of encyclopaedic knowledge.
May be barbaric but it's fun.
As the clock ticks away a lifetime,
hold your head up to the gun of a million cathode ray tubes
aimed at your tiny skull.
May you find sweet inspiration – may your memory not be dull.
May you rise to dizzy success.
May your wit be quick and strong.
May you constantly amaze us.
May your answers not be wrong.
May your head be on your shoulders.
May your tongue be in your cheek.
And most of all we pray that you may come back next week!
Be a quizz kid.
Be a whizz kid.

Crazed Institution

Just a little touch of make-up; just a little touch of bull;
just a little 3-chord trick embedded in your platform soul;
you can wear a gold Piaget on your Semaphore wrist;
you can dance the old adage with a new dapper twist.
And you can ring a crown of roses round your cranium,
live and die upon your cross of platinum.
Join the crazed institution of the stars.
Be the man that you think (know) you really are.

Crawl inside your major triad, curl up and laugh
as your agent scores another front page photograph.
Is it them or is it you throwing dice inside the loo
awaiting someone else to pull the chain.
Well grab the old bog-handle, hold your breath and light a candle.
Clear your throat and pray for rain to irrigate the corridors that echo in
your brain filled with empty nothingness, empty hunger pains.

And you can ring a crown of roses round your cranium,
live and die upon your cross of platinum.
Join the crazed institution of the stars.
Be the man that you think (know) you really are.

Salamander

Salamander –
born in the sun-kissed flame.
Who was it lit your candle –
branded you with your name?
I see you walking by my window
in your Kensington haze.
Salamander, burn for me
and I'll burn for you.

Taxi Grab

Shake a leg, it's the big rush,
can't find a taxi can't find a bus.
Bodies jammed in the underground
evacuating London town.
Nowhere to put your feet
as the big store shoppers and the pavements meet.
Red lights – pin stripes – short step shuffle into the night.
Tea time calls – the Bingo Halls open at seven in the old front stalls.
How about a Taxi Grab.

There's an empty cab by the taxi stand
driver's in the café washing his hands.
Big diesel idles – the key's inside –
c'mon Sally let's take a ride.
Flag down – uptown – no sweat.
For rush hour travel, it's the best bet yet.
Taxi Grab.

From A Dead Beat To An Old Greaser

From a dead beat to an old greaser[1], here's thinking of you.
You won't remember the long nights;
coffee bars; black tights and white thighs
in shop windows where blond assistants fully-fashioned a world made
of dummies (with no mummies or daddies to reject them).
When bombs were banned[2] every Sunday and the Shadows played F.B.I.
And tired young sax-players sold their instruments of torture –
sat in the station sharing wet dreams of Charlie Parker,
Jack Kerouac, René Magritte, to name a few of the heroes
who were too wise for their own good – left the young brood to
go on living without them.

Old queers with young faces – who remember your name,
though you're a dead beat with tired feet;
two ends that don't meet.
To a dead beat from an old greaser.

Think you must have me all wrong.
I didn't care, friend. I wasn't there, friend.
If it's the price of a pint that you need, ask me again.

Bad-Eyed And Loveless

Yes'n she's bad-eyed and she's loveless.
A young man's fancy and an old man's dream.
I'm self raising and I flower in her company.
Give me no sugar without her cream.

She's a warm fart at Christmas.
She's a breath of champagne on sparkling night.
Yes'n she's bad-eyed and she's loveless.
Turns other women to envious green.
Yes'n she's bad-eyed and she's loveless.
She's a young man's vision – in my old man's dream.

1 Greaser: rocker of the seventies
2 Ban the bomb: slogan of the early disarmament movement

Big Dipper

The mist rolls off the beaches:
the train rolls into the station.
Weekend-happiness seekers – pent-up saturation.
Well, we don't mean anyone any harm,
we weren't on the Glasgow train.
See you at the Pleasure Beach:
roller-coasting heroes.
Big Dipper riding –
we'll give the local lads a hiding
if they keep us from the ladies
hanging out in the penny arcades.
Shaking up the Tower Ballroom
throwing up in the bathroom.
Landlady's in the backroom –
I'm the Big Dipper –
it's the weekend rage.

Rich widowed landlady give me your spare front door key.
If you're 39 or over, I'll make love to you next Thursday –
I may stay over for a week or two
drop a postcard to my mum.
I'll see you at the waltzer –
we'll go big-dipping daily.

Too Old To Rock'n'Roll: Too Young To Die

The old Rocker wore his hair too long,
wore his trouser cuffs too tight.
Unfashionable to the end – drank his ale too light.
Death's head belt buckle – yesterday's dreams –
the transport caf' prophet of doom.
Ringing no change in his double-sewn seams
in his post-war-babe gloom.

Now he's too old to Rock'n'Roll but he's too young to die.

He once owned a Harley Davidson and a Triumph Bonneville.
Counted his friends in burned-out spark plugs
and prays that he always will.
But he's the last of the blue blood greaser boys
all of his mates are doing time:
married with three kids up by the ring road
sold their souls straight down the line.
And some of them own little sports cars
and meet at the tennis club do's.
For drinks on a Sunday – work on Monday.
They've thrown away their blue suede shoes.

Now they're too old to Rock'n'Roll and they're too young to die.

So the old Rocker gets out his bike
to make a ton before he takes his leave.
Up on the A 1 by Scotch Corner
just like it used to be.
And as he flies – tears in his eyes –
his wind-whipped words echo the final take
and he hits the trunk road doing around 120
with no room left to brake.

And he was too old to Rock'n'Roll but he was too young to die.
No, you're never too old to Rock'n'Roll if you're too young to die.

Pied Piper

Now if you think Ray blew it,
there was nothing to it.
They patched him up as good as new.
You can see him every day –
riding down the queen's highway,
handing out his small cigars to the kids from school.
And all the little girls with their bleached blond curls
clump up on their platform soles.
And they say »Hey Ray – let's ride away
downtown where we can roll some alley bowls.«
And Ray grins from ear to here, and whispers …

So follow me. Trail along,
my leather jacket's buttoned up.
And my four-stroke song
will pick you up when your last class ends;
and you can tell all your friends:
The Pied Piper pulled you,
the mad biker fooled you,
I'll do what you want to:
If you ride with me on a Friday
anything goes.

So follow me, hold on tight.
My school girl fancy's flowing in free flight.
I've a tenner in my skin tight jeans.
You can touch it if your hands are clean.

The Pied Piper pulled you,
the mad biker fooled you,
I'll do what you want to:
If you ride with me on a Friday
anything goes.

The Chequered Flag (Dead Or Alive)

The disc brakes drag,
the chequered flag sweeps across the oil-slick track.
The young man's home; dry as a bone.
His helmet off, he waves: the crowd waves back.
One lap victory roll. Gladiator soul.
The taker of the day in winning has to say,
Isn't it grand to be playing to the stand,
dead or alive.

The sunlight streaks through the curtain cracks,
touches the old man where he sleeps.
The nurse brings up a cup of tea –
two biscuits and the morning paper mystery.
The hard road's end, the white god's-send
is nearer everyday, in dying the old man says,
Isn't it grand to be playing to the stand,
dead or alive.

The still-born child can't feel the rain
as the chequered flag falls once again.
The deaf composer completes his final score.
He'll never hear the sweet encore.
The chequered flag, the bull's red rag,
the lemming-hearted hordes
running ever faster to the shore singing,
Isn't it grand to be playing to the stand,
dead or alive.

SONGS FROM THE WOOD

February 1977

Songs From The Wood
Jack-In-The-Green
Cup Of Wonder
Hunting Girl
Ring Out, Solstice Bells
Velvet Green
The Whistler
Pibroch (Cap In Hand)
Fire At Midnight

Songs From The Wood

Let me bring you songs from the wood:
to make you feel much better than you could know.
Dust you down from tip to toe.
Show you how the garden grows.
Hold you steady as you go.
Join the chorus if you can:
it'll make of you an honest man.
Let me bring you love from the field:
poppies red and roses filled with summer rain.
To heal the wound and still the pain
that threatens again and again
as you drag down every lover's lane.
Life's long celebration's here.
I'll toast you all in penny cheer.
Let me bring you all things refined:
galliards[1] and lute songs served in chilling ale.
Greetings well met fellow, hail!
I am the wind to fill your sail.
I am the cross to take your nail:
a singer of these ageless times.
With kitchen prose and gutter rhymes.
Songs from the wood make you feel much better.

1 Galliards: dance tunes of the Renaissance

Jack-In-The-Green

Have you seen Jack-In-The-Green[1]?
With his long tail hanging down.
He quietly sits under every tree –
   in the folds of his velvet gown.
He drinks from the empty acorn cup
   the dew that dawn sweetly bestows.
And taps his cane upon the ground –
   signals the snowdrops it's time to grow.

It's no fun being Jack-In-The-Green –
   no place to dance, no time for song.
He wears the colours of the summer soldier –
   carries the green flag all winter long.

Jack, do you never sleep –
   does the green still run deep in your heart?
Or will these changing times,
   motorways, powerlines,
   keep us apart?
Well, I don't think so –
   I saw some grass growing through the pavements today.

The rowan, the oak and the holly tree
   are the charges left for you to groom.
Each blade of grass whispers Jack-In-The-Green.
Oh Jack, please help me through my winter's night.
And we are the berries on the holly tree.
Oh, the mistlethrush is coming,
Jack, put out the light.

1 Jack-In-The Green: figure in Celtic mythology; responsible for nature's awakening after a cold frosty
  winter

Cup Of Wonder

May I make my fond excuses
   for the lateness of the hour,
   but we accept your invitation, and we bring you Beltane's[1] flower.
For the May Day is the great day, sung along the old straight track.
And those who ancient lines did lay
   will heed the song that calls them back.
Pass the word and pass the lady, pass the plate to all who hunger.
Pass the wit of ancient wisdom, pass the cup of crimson wonder.

Ask the green man[2] where he comes from, ask the cup that fills with red.
Ask the old grey standing stones that show the sun its way to bed.
Question all as to their ways,
   and learn the secrets that they hold.
Walk the lines of nature's palm
   crossed with silver and with gold.
Pass the cup and pass the lady, pass the plate to all who hunger.
Pass the wit of ancient wisdom, pass the cup of crimson wonder.

Join in black December's sadness,
   lie in August's welcome corn.
Stir the cup that's ever-filling
   with the blood of all that's born.
But the May Day is the great day, sung along the old straight track.
And those who ancient lines did lay
   will heed the song that calls them back.
Pass the word and pass the lady, pass the plate to all who hunger.
Pass the wit of ancient wisdom, pass the cup of crimson wonder.

1 Beltane: Celtic festival of fire in which all fires in the houses were extinguished and then rekindled with
  the flame of a holy fire (from the Gaelic *Bealltainn*, 1st of May)
2 The green man: refer to footnote in *Jack-In-The-Green*

Hunting Girl

One day I walked the road and crossed a field
    to go by where the hounds ran hard.
And on the master raced: behind the hunters chased
    to where the path was barred.
One fine young lady's horse refused the fence to clear.
I unlocked the gate but she did wait until the pack had disappeared.

Crop handle carved in bone;
    sat high upon a throne of finest English leather.
The queen of all the pack,
    this joker raised his hat and talked about the weather.
All should be warned about this high born Hunting Girl.
She took this simple man's downfall in hand;
    I raised the flag that she unfurled.

Boot leather flashing and spurnecks the size of my thumb.
This highborn hunter had tastes as strange as they come.
Unbridled passion: I took the bit in my teeth.
Her standing over – me on my knees underneath.

My lady, be discreet.
I must get to my feet and go back to the farm.
Whilst I appreciate you are no deviate,
    I might come to some harm.
I'm not inclined to acts refined, if that's how it goes.
Oh high born Hunting Girl
    I'm just a normal low born so and so.

Ring Out, Solstice Bells

Now is the solstice of the year,
    winter is the glad song that you hear.
Seven maids move in seven time.
Have the lads up ready in a line.

Ring out these bells.
Ring out, ring solstice bells.
Ring solstice bells.

Join together beneath the mistletoe,
    by the holy oak whereon it grows.
Seven druids dance in seven time.
Sing the song the bells call, loudly chiming.

Ring out these bells.
Ring out, ring solstice bells.
Ring solstice bells.

Praise be to the distant sister sun,
    joyful as the silver planets run.
Seven maids move in seven time.
Sing the song of bells call, loudly chiming.
Ring out those bells.
Ring out, ring solstice bells.
Ring solstice bells.
Ring on, ring out.
Ring on, ring out.

Velvet Green

Walking on velvet green. Scots pine growing.
Isn't it rare to be taking the air, singing.
Walking on velvet green.
Walking on velvet green. Distant cows lowing.
Never a care: with your legs in the air, loving.
Walking on velvet green.
Won't you have my company, yes, take it in your hands.
Go down on velvet green, with a country man.
Who's a young girls fancy and an old maid's dream.
Tell your mother that you walked all night on velvet green.
One dusky half-hour's ride up to the north.
There lies your reputation and all that you're worth.
Where the scent of wild roses turns the milk to cream.
Tell your mother that you walked all night on velvet green.
And the long grass blows in the evening cool.
And August's rare delights may be April's fool.
But think not of that, my love,
I'm tight against the seam.
And I'm growing up to meet you down on velvet green.
Now I may tell you that it's love and not just lust.
And if we live the lie, let's lie in trust.
On golden daffodils, to catch the silver stream
that washes out the wild oat seed on velvet green.
We'll dream as lovers under the stars –
of civilizations raging afar.
And the ragged dawn breaks on your battle scars.
As you walk home cold and alone upon velvet green.
Walking on velvet green. Scots pine growing.
Isn't it rare to be taking the air, singing.
Walking on velvet green.
Walking on velvet green. Distant cows lowing.
Never a care: with your legs in the air, loving.
Walking on velvet green.

The Whistler

I'll buy you six bay mares to put in your stable –
six golden apples bought with my pay.
I am the first piper who calls the sweet tune,
but I must be gone by the seventh day.

So come on, I'm the whistler.
I have a fife and a drum to play.
Get ready for the whistler.
I whistle along on the seventh day –
whistle along on the seventh day.

All kinds of sadness I've left behind me.
Many's the day when I have done wrong.
But I'll be yours for ever and ever.
Climb in the saddle and whistle along.

So come on, I'm the whistler.
I have a fife and a drum to play.
Get ready for the whistler.
I whistle along on the seventh day –
whistle along on the seventh day.

Deep red are the sun-sets in mystical places.
Black are the nights on summer-day sands.
We'll find the speck of truth in each riddle.
Hold the first grain of love in our hands.

Pibroch[1] (Cap In Hand)

There's a light in the house in the wood in the valley.
There's a thought in the head of the man.
Who carries his dreams like the coat slung on his shoulder.
Bringing you love in the cap in his hand.
And each step he takes is one half of a lifetime:
no word he would say could you understand.
So he bundles his regrets into a gesture of sorrow.
Bringing you love cap in hand.
Catching breath as he looks through the dining-room window:
candle lit table for two has been laid.
Strange slippers by the fire.
Strange boots in the hallway.
Put my cap on my head.
I turn and walk away.

Fire At Midnight

I believe in fires at midnight –
   when the dogs have all been fed.
A golden toddy on the mantle –
   a broken gun beneath the bed.
Silken mist outside the window.
Frogs and newts slip in the dark –
   too much hurry ruins the body.
I'll sit easy … fan the spark
   kindled by the dying embers of another working day.
Go upstairs … take off your makeup –
   fold your clothes neatly away.
Me, I'll sit and write this love song
   as I all too seldom do –
   build a little fire this midnight.
It's good to be back home with you.

Pibroch (gaelic): piece of music for Scottish bagpipes

REPEAT – THE BEST OF JETHRO TULL VOL. II

November 1977

Minstrel In The Gallery (*Minstrel In The Gallery*)
Cross-Eyed Mary (*Aqualung*)
A New Day Yesterday (*Stand Up*)
Bourée (*Stand Up*)
Thick As A Brick Edit # 4 (*Thick As A Brick*)
WarChild (*WarChild*)
A Passion Play Edit # 9 (*A Passion Play*)
To Cry You A Song (*Benefit*)
Too Old To Rock'n'Roll … (*Too Old To Rock'n'Roll …*)
Glory Row

Glory Row

Rise up all you fine young ladies and take arms for the show.
Oh, we'll put your name up in lights,
put you down on Glory Row.
Would you be the star of ages
to light your own way at night?
Might be a former beauty queen with your high smile stuck on so tightly.
They come and they go down on Glory Row.
It's the same old story – yes, it's the same old show.

Well, hello all you gentlemen, I fear I'm a lot like you.
We're wearing the same school tie but a different pair of shoes.
How did you get to be who you are?
Will your children share the blame?
Is it really worth the time it takes
to carve your name on Glory Row?

Down on Glory Row.
It's the same old story – yes, it's the same old show.

HEAVY HORSES

January 1978

… And The Mouse Police Never Sleeps
Acres Wild
No Lullaby
Moths
Journeyman
Rover
One Brown Mouse
Heavy Horses
Weathercock

... And The Mouse Police Never Sleeps

Muscled, black with steel-green eye
    swishing through the rye grass
    with thoughts of mouse-and-apple pie.
Tail balancing at half-mast.
... And the mouse police never sleeps –
    lying in the cherry tree.
Savage bed foot-warmer of purest feline ancestry.
Look out, little furry folk!
He's the all-night working cat.
Eats but one in every ten –
    leaves the others on the mat.
... And the mouse police never sleeps –
    waiting by the cellar door.
Window-box town crier;
    birth and death registrar.
With claws that rake a furrow red –
    licensed to mutilate.
From warm milk on a lazy day
    to dawn patrol on hungry hate.
... No, the mouse police never sleeps –
    climbing on the ivy.
Windy roof-top weathercock.
Warm-blooded night on a cold tile.

Acres Wild

I'll make love to you
  in all good places
  under black mountains
  in open spaces.
By deep brown rivers
  that slither darkly
  through far marches
  where the blue hare races.

Come with me to the Winged Isle[1] –
  northern father's western child.
Where the dance of ages is playing still
  through far marches of acres wild.

I'll make love to you
  in narrow side streets
  with shuttered windows,
  crumbling chimneys.

Come with me to the weary town –
  discos silent under tiles
  that slide from roof-tops, scatter softly
  on concrete marches of acres wild.

By red bricks pointed
  with cement fingers.
Flaking damply from sagging shoulders.

Come with me to the Winged Isle –
  northern father's western child.
Where the dance of ages is playing still
  through far marches of acres wild.

1 Winged Isle: Isle of Skye, Scotland

No Lullaby

Keep your eyes open and prick up your ears –
    rehearse your loudest cry.
There's folk out there who would do you harm
    so I'll sing you no lullaby.
There's a lock on the window; there's a chain on the door:
    a big dog in the hall.
But there's dragons and beasties out there in the night
    to snatch you if you fall.

So come out fighting with your rattle in hand.
Thrust and parry. Light
    a match to catch the devil's eye. Bring
    a cross of fire to the fight.

And let no sleep bring false relief
    from the tension of the fray.
Come wake the dead with the scream of life.
Do battle with the ghosts at play.

Gather your toys at the call-to-arms
    and swing your big bear down.
Upon our necks when we come to set
    you sleeping safe and sound.

It's as well we tell no lie
    to chase the face that cries.
And little birds can't fly
    so keep an open eye.
It's as well we tell no lie
    so I'll sing you no lullaby.

Moths

The leaded window opened
    to move the dancing candle flame
And the first moths of summer
    suicidal came.
And a new breeze chattered
    in its May-bud tenderness –
Sending water-lilies sailing
    as she turned to get undressed.
And the long night awakened
    and we soared on powdered wings –
Circling our tomorrows
    in the wary month of Spring.
Chasing shadows slipping
    in a magic lantern slide –
Creatures of the candle
    on a night-light-ride.
Dipping and weaving – flutter
    through the golden needle's eye
    in our haystack madness. Butterfly-stroking
    on a Spring-tide high.
Life's too long (as the Lemming said)
    as the candle burned and the moths were wed.
And we'll all burn together as the wick grows higher –
    before the candle's dead.
The leaded window opened
    to move the dancing candle flame.
And the first moths of summer
    suicidal came
    to join in the worship
    of the light that never dies
    in a moment's reflection
    of two moths spinning in her eyes.

Journeyman

Spine-tingling railway sleepers –
Sleepy houses lying four-square and firm
Orange beams divide the darkness
Rumbling fit to turn the waking worm.
Sliding through Victorian tunnels
    where green moss oozes from the pores.
Dull echoes from the wet embankments –
Battlefield allotments. Fresh open sores.

In late night commuter madness
Double-locked black briefcase on the floor
    like a faithful dog with master
      sleeping in the draught beside the carriage door.
To each journeyman his own home-coming
Cold supper nearing with each station stop
Frosty flakes on empty platforms
Fireside slippers waiting. Flip. Flop.

Journeyman night-tripping on the late fantastic
Too late to stop for tea at Gerard's Cross
    and hear the soft shoes on the footbridge shuffle
      as the wheels turn biting on the midnight frost.
On the late commuter special
Carriage lights that flicker, fade and die
Howling into hollow blackness
Dusky diesel shudders in full cry.
Down redundant morning papers
Abandon crosswords with a cough
Stationmaster in his wisdom
    told the guard to turn the heating off.

Rover

I chase your every footstep
    and I follow every whim.
When you call the tune I'm ready
    to strike up the battle hymn.
My lady of the meadows –
My comber of the beach –
You've thrown the stick for your dog's trick
    but it's floating out of reach.
The long road is a rainbow and the pot of gold lies there.
So slip the chain and I'm off again –
You'll find me everywhere. I'm a Rover.

As the robin craves the summer
    to hide his smock of red,
I need the pillow of your hair
    in which to hide my head.
I'm simple in my sadness,
    resourceful in remorse.
Then I'm down straining at the lead –
    holding on a windward course.

Strip me from the bundle
    of balloons at every fair:
    colourful and carefree –
Designed to make you stare.
But I'm lost and I'm losing
    the thread that holds me down.
And I'm up hot and rising
    in the lights of every town.

One Brown Mouse

Smile your little smile – take some tea with me awhile.
Brush away that black cloud from your shoulder.
Twitch your whiskers. Feel that you're really real.
Another tea-time – another day older.

Puff warm breath on your tiny hands.
You wish you were a man
      who every day can turn another page.
Behind your glass you sit and look
      at my ever-open book –
One brown mouse sitting in a cage.

Do you wonder if I really care for you –
Am I just the company you keep –
Which one of us exercises on the old treadmill –
Who hides his head, pretending to sleep?

Smile your little smile – take some tea with me awhile.
Brush away that black cloud from your shoulder.
Twitch your whiskers. Feel that you're really real.
Another tea-time – another day older.

Smile your little smile – take some tea with me awhile.
And every day we'll turn another page.
Behind our glass we'll sit and look
      at our ever-open book –
One brown mouse sitting in a cage.

Heavy Horses

Iron-clad feather-feet pounding the dust
An October's day, towards evening
Sweat embossed veins standing proud to the plough
Salt on a deep chest seasoning
Last of the line at an honest day's toil
Turning the deep sod under
Flint at the fetlock, chasing the bone
Flies at the nostrils plunder.

The Suffolk, the Clydesdale, the Percheron[1] vie
    with the Shire[2] on his feathers floating
Hauling soft timber into the dusk
    to bed on a warm straw coating.

Heavy horses, move the land under me
Behind the plough gliding – slipping and sliding free
Now you're down to the few
And there's no work to do
The tractor's on its way.

Let me find you a filly for your proud stallion seed
    to keep the old line going
And we'll stand you abreast at the back of the wood
    behind the young trees growing
To hide you from eyes that mock at your girth,
    and your eighteen hands at the shoulder
And one day when the oil barons have all dripped dry
    and the nights are seen to draw colder
They'll beg for your strength, your gentle power
    your noble grace and your bearing
And you'll strain once again to the sound of the gulls
    in the wake of the deep plough, sharing.

Standing like tanks on the brow of the hill
Up into the cold wind facing
In stiff battle harness, chained to the world
Against the low sun racing

1 Suffolk, Clydesdale, Percheron: all breeds of heavy horses
2 Shire: largest breed of heavy horse; used as warhorse in medieval times

Bring me a wheel of oaken wood
A rein of polished leather
A heavy horse and a tumbling sky
Brewing heavy weather.

Bring a song for the evening
Clean brass to flash the dawn
   across these acres glistening
   like dew on a carpet lawn
In these dark towns folks lie sleeping
   as the heavy horses thunder by
   to wake the dying city
   with the living horseman's cry
At once the old hands quicken –
   bring pick and wisp and curry comb –
   thrill to the sound of all
   the heavy horses coming home.

Weathercock

Good morning Weathercock: How did you fare last night?
Did the cold wind bite you, did you face up to the fright
When the leaves spin from October
   and whip around your tail?
Did you shake from the blast, did you shiver through the gale?

Give us direction; the best of goodwill –
Put us in touch with fair winds.
Sing to us softly, hum evening's song –
Tell us what the blacksmith has done for you.

Do you simply reflect changes in the patterns of the sky,
Or is it true to say the weather heeds the twinkle in your eye?
Do you fight the rush of winter; and you hold snowflakes at bay?
Do you lift the dawn sun from the fields and help him on his way?

Good morning Weathercock: make this day bright.
Put us in touch with your fair winds.
Sing to us softly, hum evening's song.
Point the way to better days we can share with you.

STORMWATCH

September 1979

North Sea Oil
Orion
Home
Dark Ages
Warm Sporran (Instrumental)
Something's On The Move
Old Ghosts
Dun Ringill
Flying Dutchman
Elegy (Instrumental / David Palmer)

North Sea Oil

Black and viscous – bound to cure blue lethargy
Sugar-plum petroleum for energy
Tightrope-balanced payments need a small reprieve
Oh, please believe we want to be
    in North Sea Oil
New-found wealth sits on the shelf of yesterday
Hot-air balloon – inflation soon will make you pay
Riggers rig and diggers dig their shallow grave
But we'll be saved and what we crave
    is North Sea Oil
Prices boom in Aberdeen and London Town
Ten more years to lay the fears, erase the frown
    before we are all nuclear – the better way!
Oh, let us pray: we want to stay
    in North Sea Oil

Orion

Orion, won't you give me your star sign
Orion, get up on the sky-line
I'm high on my hill and I feel fine
Orion, let's sip the heaven's heady wine

Orion, light your lights:
    come guard the open spaces
    from the black horizon to the pillow where I lie.
Your faithful dog shines brighter than its lord and master
Your jewelled sword twinkles as the world rolls by.
So come up singing above the cloudy cover
Stare through at people who toss fitful in their sleep.
I know you're watching as the old gent by the station
    scuffs his toes on old fag packets lying in the street
And silver shadows flick across the closing bistro.
Sweet waiters link their arms and patter down the street,
    their words lost blowing on cold winds in darkest Chelsea.
Prime years fly fading with each young heart's beat

Orion, won't you make me a star sign
Orion, get up on the sky-line
I'm high on your love and I feel fine
Orion, let's sip the heaven's heady wine

And young girls shiver as they wait by lonely bus-stops
    after sad parties: no-one to take them home
    to greasy bed-sitters and make a late-night play
    for lost virginity a thousand miles away

Home

As the dawn sun breaks over sleepy gardens
    I'll be here to do all things to comfort you.
And though I've been away
    left you alone this way
    why don't you come awake
    and let your first smile take me home.
The shadows in the park were longer yesterday
    and Lady Luck stood still, waiting for the kill.
And on a jumbo ride
    over seas grey, deep and wide
    I flew for heaven's sake
    and let the angels take me home.
Down steep and narrow lanes I see the chimneys smoking
    above the golden fields … know what the robin feels
    in his summer jamboree.
All elements agree
    in sweet and stormy blend –
    midwife to winds that send me home.

Dark Ages

Darlings are you ready for the long winter's fall?
    said the lady in her parlor
    said the butler in the hall.
Is there time for another?
    cried the drunkard in his sleep.
Not likely
    said the little child. What's done
    the Lord can keep.
And the vicar stands a-praying.
And the television dies
    as the white dot flickers and is gone
    and no-one stops to cry.

The big jet rumbles over runway miles
    that scar the patchwork green
    where slick tycoons and rich buffoons
    have opened up the seam
    of golden nights and champagne flights
    ad-man overkill
    and in the haze
    consumer crazed
    we take the sugar pill.
Jagged fires mark the picket lines
    the politicians weep
    and mealy-mouthed
    down corridors of power on tip-toe creep.
Come and see bureaucracy
    make its final heave
    and let the new disorder through
    while senses take their leave.
Families screaming line the streets
    and put the windows through
    in corner shops
    where keepers kept
    the country's life-blood blue.
Take their pick
    and try the trick
    with loaves and fishes shared
    and the vicar shouts
    as the lights go out,
    and no-one really cares.

Dark Ages
    shaking the dead
Closed pages
    better not read
Cold rages
    burn in your head.

Something's On The Move

She wore a black tiara
   rare gems upon her fingers
   and she came from distant waters
   where northern lights explode
   to celebrate the dawning
   of the new wastes of winter
   gathering royal momentum
   on the icy road.
With chill mists swirling
   like petticoats in motion
   sighted on horizons
   for ten thousand years
   the lady of the ice sounds
   a deathly distant rumble
   to Titanic-breaking children lost
   in melting crystal tears.
Capturing black pieces
   in a glass-fronted museum
   the white queen rolls
   on the chessboard of the dawn
   squeezing through the valleys
   pausing briefly in the corries
   the Ice-Mother mates
   and a new age is born.
Driving all before her
   un-stoppable, un-straining
   her cold creaking mass
   follows reindeer down.
Thin spreading fingers seek
   to embrace the sill-warm bundles
   that huddle on the doorsteps
   of a white London Town.
Oh, sunshine – take me now away from here
I'm a needle on a spiral in a groove.
And the turntable spins
   as the last waltz begins
And the weather-man says
   something's on the move.

Old Ghosts

Hair stands high on the cat's back like
　　a ridge of threatening hills.
Sheepdogs howl, make tracks and growl –
　　their tails hanging low.
And young children falter in their games
　　at the altar of life's hide-and-seek
　　between tall pillars, where Sunday-night killers
　　in grey raincoats peek.

Misty colours unfold a backcloth cold –
　　fine tapestry of silk
I draw around me like a cloak
　　and soundless glide a-drifting
　　on eddies whirled in beech leaves furled –
　　brown and gold they fly
　　in the warm mesh of sunlight
　　sifting now from a cloudless sky.

I'll be coming again like an old dog in pain
Blown through the eye of a hurricane
Down to the stones where old ghosts play.

Dun Ringill

Clear light on a slick palm
    as I mis-deal the day
Slip the night from a shaved pack
    make a marked card play
Call twilight hours down
    from a heaven home
    high above the highest bidder
    for the good Lord's throne
In the wee hours I'll meet you
    down by Dun Ringill[1] –
    oh, and we'll watch the old gods play
    by Dun Ringill
We'll wait in stone circles
    'til the force comes through –
    lines join in faint discord
    and the stormwatch brews
    a concert of kings
    as the white sea snaps
    at the heels of a soft prayer
    whispered
In the wee hours I'll meet you
    down by Dun Ringill –
    oh, and I'll take you quickly
    by Dun Ringill

1 Dun Ringill: small historical fortress on the Isle of Skye, Scotland

Flying Dutchman

Old lady with a barrow: life near ending
Standing by the harbour wall: warm wishes sending
    children on the cold sea swell –
    not fishers of men –
    gone to chase away the last herring:
    come empty home again.
So come all you lovers of the good life
    on your supermarket run –
Set a sail of your own devising
    and be there when the Dutchman comes.
Wee girl in a straw hat: from far east warring
Sad cargo of an old ship: young bodies whoring
Slow ocean hobo – ports closed to her crew
No hope of immigration – keep on passing through.
So come all you lovers of the good life
    your children playing in the sun –
    set a sympathetic flag a-flying
    and be there when the Dutchman comes.

Death grinning like a scarecrow – Flying Dutchman[1]
Seagull pilots flown from nowhere – try and touch one
    as she slips in on the full tide
    and the harbour-master yells
All hands vanished with the captain –
    no one left, the tale to tell.

So come all you lovers of the good life
Look around you, can you see?
Staring ghostly from the mirror –
    it's the Dutchman you will be
… floating slowly out to sea
    in a misty misery.

1 Flying Dutchman: figure from an old sea-saga; Dutch captain, damned to sail in all eternity

A

September 1980

Crossfire
Fylingdale Flyer
Working John, Working Joe
Black Sunday
Protect And Survive
Batteries Not Included
Uniform
4.W.D. (Low Ratio)
The Pine Marten's Jig (Instrumental)
And Further On

Crossfire

Spring light in a hazy May
and a man with a gun at the door
Someone's crawling on the roof above –
    all the media here for the show
I've been waiting for our friends to come
Like spiders down ropes to free-fall
A thirty round clip for a visiting card –
    admit one to the embassy ball

Caught in the crossfire on Princes Gate Avenue[1]
In go the windows and out go the lights
Call me a doctor. Fetch me a policeman
I'm down on the floor in one hell of a fight

I'm just a soul with an innocent face –
    a regular boy dressed in blue
    conducting myself in a proper way
    as befitting the job that I do
They came down on me like a ton of bricks
Swept off my feet, knocked about
There's nothing for it but to sit and wait
    for the hard men to get me out

Calm reason floats from the street below
    and the slow fuse burns through the night
Everyone's tried to talk it through
    but they can't seem to get the deal right
Somewhere there are Brownings[2] in a two-hand hold –
    cocked and locked, one up the spout
There's nothing for it but to sit and wait
    for the hard men to get me out

1 ... caught in the crossfire: refers to the freeing of hostages out of the Iranian embassy in London
2 Browning: pistol named after its American inventor

Fylingdale Flyer

Through clear skies tracking lightly from far down the line
No fanfare, just a blip on the screen
No quick conclusions now – everything will be fine
Short-circuit glitsch and not what it seems
Fylingdale Flyer[1] – you're only half way there
Green screen liar –
For a second or so we were running scared

On late shift, feeling drowsy eyes glued to the display
Dead cert alert, lit match to the straw
One last quick game of bowls – we can still win the day
Fail-safe; forget the things that you saw

They checked the systems through and they read A - o.k.
Some tiny fuse has probably blown
Sit back; relax and soon it will just go away
Keep your hands off that red telephone

1 Fylingdales: site of the British early warning system

Working John, Working Joe

When I was a young man (as all good tales begin)
    I was taught to hold out my hand
And for my pay I worked an honest day
    and took what pittance I could win
Now I'm a working John and I'm a working Joe
    and I'm doing what I know
    for God and the Economy
Big brother watches over me
And the state protects and feeds me
And my conscience never leaves me
And I'm loyal to the unions
    who protect me at all levels

And as I grew, the winds of fortune blew
    and the bank smiled down upon me
And mortgaged to the hilt I threw
    the breeze of caution behind me
Now I'm a working John and I'm a working Joe
    and I'm good at what I know
And God and the Economy
    have blessed me with equality
Now I'm equal to the best of you
And better than the rest of you
    who would criticise my success
    in times of national unrest

Now I own my horseless carriage
    in its central-heated garage
And I commute eighty miles a day –
    up at seven to make it pay
I direct ten limited companies
    with seeming consummate expertise
    two ulcers and a heart disease
    a trembling feeling in both knees –
I'm a working John and I'm a working Joe

Black Sunday

Tomorrow is the one day I would change for a Monday
    with freezing rains melting and no trains running
    and sad eyes passing in windows flimsy
    and my seat rocking from legs not quite matching
Got passport, credit cards, a plane that I'm catching
Black Sunday falls one day too soon

The taxi that takes me will be moving so quickly
My suitcases simply too full for the closing
    of pants, shirts and kisses all packed in a hurry
Two best-selling paper backs chosen at random –
    no sign of sales-persons to whom I might hand them
Black Sunday falls one day too soon

And down at the airport are probably waiting
    a few thousand passengers, overbooked seating
Time long suspended in transit-lounge traumas –
    connection broken and Special Branch waiting
    conspicuously standing in holiday clothing
Black Sunday falls one day too soon

Pick up my feet and kick off my lethargy
Down to the gate with the old mood upon me
Get out and chase the small immortality
    born in the minute of my next returning
Impatient feet tapping and cigarette burning
Homecoming one day too soon

And back at the house there's a grey sky a-tumbling
Milk bottles piling on doorsteps a-crumbling
Curtains all drawn and cold water plumbing
Notepaper scribbles I read unbelieving
Saying how sorry, how sad was the leaving
… one day too soon

Protect And Survive

They said protect and you'll survive[1] –
    (but our postman didn't call)
8lbs. of over-pressure wave seemed to glue him to the wall
They said protect and you'll survive

E.M.P.[2] took out the radio –
    (and our milk-man didn't call)
Flash blinded by the pretty lights,
    didn't see his bottles fall
    or feel the warm black rain arrive

Big friendly cloud builds in the West
    (and our dust-men haven't called)
They left the dual carriageway at a hundred miles an hour –
    a tail wind chasing them away

And in deep shelters lurk below, sub-regional control
    who sympathise but cannot help
    to mend your body or your soul
Self-appointed guardians of the race with egg upon their face
When steady sirens sing all-clear they pop up,
    find nobody here

And so I watch two new suns spin –
    (our paper man doesn't call)
Burnt shadow printed on the road – now there's nothing there at all
They said protect and you'll survive

1 Protect And Survive: brochure issued by the British government, listing precautions to be taken in the
  event of a nuclear attack
2 E.M.P.: electro magnetic pulse after a nuclear explosion, which renders electric equipment useless

Batteries Not Included

Six o'clock in the morning
Wake up by the bed
There sits a new Japanese toy
And I like it
See the name on the wrapping
Can't read yet but I know
    it's made for me (lucky boy)
And I want it
Lights that flash, wheels that go round
Digital display
Fresh silicon chips to enjoy
And I need them
(Where's the batteries?)
Sitting silent and empty
Wish I could breathe life
    in my new friend who's terribly still
And I like him
Just like me. P'rhaps he's hungry.
Six volts make him smile
And twelve volts would probably kill
How I like him
    Daddy, where's the batteries
    I can't find my batteries
(There's no batteries)
Seven o'clock in the morning
They find me by the bed
    with my friend the Japanese toy
I am with him
Mummy, Daddy – can't see you,
    hear you. Batteries not
    included in this little boy
(Where's my batteries?)

Uniform

See black, see yellow with little notebooks drawn
See grey stripes bowling down the street
Silver streaks and T-shirts so precisely torn
Strange foreign chaps in white bed-sheets –
Uniforms

See golden halo'd men of high renown
    prance to the politicians' beat
Well tailored in unswerving elegance
    with shoes by Gucci on their feet –
Uniforms

How do you know who the hell you are?
Wake up each day under a different star
Dressed to the nines, meet yourself going home
    like a clone, smartly dressed in your pressed uniform

White battle dress on green pitch, proud eleven
Beneath the swelling box so neat
    the teeming millions of the future fly –
    the spinning cricket ball to cheat
They're all uniform

4.W.D. (Low Ratio)

Met a man just the other day –
    said his name was Jim. Boy, won't you take a look!
Got a car for you – it's a real steal
Cleaned it right down – new brakes, clutch and here's the hook
Yes, it's a 4.W.D. (low ratio)

Cash to Jim. I took it home
    through the deep mud. Plugged happy as a boy in sand
Fitted wide tyres, spotlight, a winch as well
    and some brush bars up in front to complete the plan
Now it's really a 4.W.D. (low ratio)

Take you down to the edge of town
Where the road stops, we start to hold the ground
Well, I'm blessed! Got traction in a special way
Hold the roll bar, slide back, feel me pull it round
Let me show you my 4.W.D. (low ratio)

And Further On

We saw the heavens break and all the world go down to sleep
    and rocks on mossy banks drip acid rain from craggy steeps
Saw fiery angels kiss the dawn
Wish you goodbye till further on
Will you still be there further on?

And troubled dynasties, like legions lost, have blown away
Hounds hard upon their heels call to their quarry – wait and play
Before the last faint light has gone
Wish you goodbye till further on
Will you still be there further on?

The angry waves grow high – cut icy teeth on northern shores
Brave fires they flicker, cough – give way to winds
    through broken doors
And with the last line almost drawn – wish you goodbye till further on
Will you still be there further on?

THE BROADSWORD AND THE BEAST

April 1982

Side 1:   Beastie

        Beastie
        Clasp
        Fallen On Hard Times
        Flying Colours
        Slow Marching Band

Side 2:   Broadsword

        Broadsword
        Pussy Willow
        Watching Me Watching You
        Seal Driver
        Cheerio

Beastie

From early days of infancy, through trembling years
of youth, long murky middle-age and final hours
long in the tooth, he's the hundred names of terror –
creature you love the least. Picture his name before
you and exorcise the beast.

He roved up and down through history – spectre
with tales to tell. In the darkness when the
campfire's dead – to each his private hell. If you look
behind your shoulder as you feel his eyes to feast, you
can witness now the everchanging nature of the beast.

Beastie

If you wear a warmer sporran, you can keep the foe at
bay. You can pop those pills and visit some
psychiatrist who'll say – There's nothing I can do
for you, everywhere's a danger zone. I'd love to help
get rid of it, but I've got one of my own.

There's a beast upon my shoulder and a fiend upon
my back. Feel his burning breath a heaving, smoke
oozing from his stack. And he moves beneath the
covers or he lies below the bed. He's the beast upon
your shoulder. He's the price upon your head. He's
the lonely fear of dying, and for some, of living too.
He's your private nightmare pricking. He'd just love
to turn the screw. So stand as one defiant – yes, and
let your voices swell. Stare that beastie in the face
and really give him hell.

The Clasp

We travellers on the endless wastes in single orbits,
gliding cold-eyed march towards the dawn behind
hard-weather hoods a-hiding.
Meeting as the tall ships do, passing in the channel
afraid to chance a gentle touch –
afraid to make the clasp.

In high rise city canyons dwells the discontent of ages.
On ring roads, nose to bumber crawl
commuters in their cages. Cryptic signals flash
across from pilots in the fast lane. Double-locked
and belted in – too late to make the clasp.

Let's break the journey now on some lonely road.
Sit down as strangers will, let the stress unload.
Talk in confidential terms, share a dark unspoken fear.
Refill the cup and drink it up. Say goodnight and
wish good luck.

Synthetic chiefs with frozen smiles holding unsteady courses.
Grip the reins of history, high on their battle horses.
And meeting as good statesmen do before the T.V.
eyes of millions, hand to hand exchange the lie –
pretend to make the clasp.

Fallen On Hard Times

Fallen on hard times – but it feels good to know
that milk and honey's just around the bend.
Running on bad lines – we'd better run as we go.
Tear up, tear up the overdraft again.

Oh, dear Prime Minister – it's all such a mess.
Go right ahead and pull the rotten tooth.
Oh, Mr. President – you've been put to the test.
Come clean, for once and hit us with the truth.

Looking for sunshine – oh but it's black and it's cold.
Yet you say that milk and honey's just around the bend.
Giving us a hard time my friends,
handing us the same line again.

Fallen on hard times – and there's nowhere to hide.
Now they've re-possessed the Rolls Royce and the mink.

Turning on the peace sign – and it's back to the wood.
Soon there will be raised a holy stink.

Somebody wake me. I've been sleeping too long.
Oh, I don't have to take this lying down.
You can keep your promises. Shove 'em where they belong.
Don't ask me to the party – won't be around.

Flying Colours

Shout if you will, but that just won't do.
I, for one, would rather follow softer options.
I'll take the easy line; another sip of wine,
and if I ignore the face you wore it's just a way of
mine to keep from flying colours.

Don't lay your bait while the whole world waits
around to see me shoot you down – it's all so second-rate.
When we can last for days on a loving night;
or for hours at least on a warm whisper given.
You always pick the best time to rise to the fight.
To break the hard bargain that we've driven.
Once again we're flying colours.

I thought we had it out the night before,
and settled old scores, but not the hard way.
Was it a glass too much? Or a smile too few?
Did our friends all catch the needle match – did we
want them to?
In a fancy restaurant we were all aglow
keeping cool by mutual permission.
How did the conversation get to where we came to blows?
We were set up in a red condition
and again we're flying colours.

Shout – but you see it still won't do.
With my colours on I can be just as bad as you.
Have I had a glass too much? Did I give a smile too few?
Did our friends all catch the needle match – did we
want them to?
We act our parts so well, like we wrote the play.
All so predictable and we know it.

We'll settle old scores now, and settle the hard way.
You may not even live to outgrow it!
Once again we're flying colours.

Slow Marching Band

Would you join a slow marching band?
And take pleasure in your leaving
as the ferry sails and tears are dried
and cows come home at evening.

Could you get behind a slow marching band?
And join together in the passing
of all we shared through yesterdays
in sorrows neverlasting.

Take a hand and take a bow.
You played for me; that's all for now, oh, and never
mind the words just hum along and keep on going.
Walk on slowly – don't look behind you.
Don't say goodbye, love. I won't remind you.

Dream of me as the nights draw cold
still marking time through Winter.
You paid the piper and called the tune
and you marched the band away.

Take a hand and take a bow.
You played for me; that's all for now, oh, and never
mind the words just hum along and keep on going.
Walk on slowly – don't look behind you.
Don't say goodbye, love. I won't remind you.

Broadsword

I see a dark sail on the horizon set under a black
cloud that hides the sun.

Bring me my broadsword and clear understanding.
Bring me my cross of gold as a talisman.
Get up to the roundhouse on the cliff-top standing.
Take women and children and bed them down.

Bring me my broadsword and clear understanding.
Bring me my cross of gold as a talisman.
Bless with a hard heart those who surround me.
Bless the women and children who firm our hands.
Put our backs to the north wind. Hold fast by the river.
Sweet memories to drive us on for the motherland.

Pussy Willow

In the half-tone light of a young morning
she sighs and shifts on the pillow.
And across her face dancing, the first shadows fly
to kiss the Pussy Willow.

In her fairy-tale world she's a lost soul singing
in a sad voice nobody hears.
She waits in her castle of make-believe
for her white knight to appear.

Pussy Willow – down fur-lined avenue
brushing the sleep from her young woman eyes.
Runs for the train – see, eight o'clock's coming
cutting dreams down to size again.

Pussy Willow – down fur-lined avenue
brushing the sleep from her young woman eyes.
Runs from the train. Hear her typewriter humming
cutting dreams down to size again.

She longs for the East and a pale dress flowing
an appartment in old Mayfair.
Or to fish the Spey, spinning the first run of Spring
or to die for a cause somewhere.

Pussy Willow – down fur-lined avenue
brushing the sleep from her young woman eyes.
Runs from the train. Hear her typewriter humming
cutting dreams down to size again.

Watching Me Watching You

I sit by the cutting on the Beaconsfield line.
He's watching me watching the trains go by,
and they move so fast – boy, they really fly.
He's still watching me watching you watching the
trains go by.

And the way he stares – feel like locking my door
and pulling my phone from the wall.
His eyes, like lights from a laser, burn
making my hair stand – making the goose-bumps crawl.

He's watching me watching you watching him
watching me
I'm watching you watching him watching me
watching Stares.

At the cocktail party with a Bucks Fizz in my hand
I feel him watching me watching the girls go by.
And they move so smooth without even trying.
He's still watching me watching you watching the
trains go by.

And the crowd thins and he moves up close but he doesn't speak.
I have to look the other way.
But curiosity gets the better part of me and I peek:
Got two drinks in his hand – see his lips move –
what the hell's he trying to say.

He's watching me watching you watching him
watching me.
I'm watching you watching him watching me
watching Stares.
He's watching me watching you watching him
watching me.
He's watching me watching you watching
the trains go by.
He's watching me watching you watching him
watching me.
He's watching me watching you watching him watching me.
He's watching me watching you watching him watching me watching him watching.

185

Seal Driver

Take you away for my magic ship.
I have two hundred diesel horses thundering loud.
Sea birds call your name and the mountain's on fire
as the summer lightning cuts the sky like a hot wire.
And you ride on the swell and your heart is alive,
think I'll make you my seal driver.

I'm no great looker, I'm no fast shakes.
I'll give you a steady push on a six knot simmering
high tide.
I can hold us down – keep our head to the wind,
or let us roll on the broadside, cold spray flying in,
and we'll ride on the swell and our hearts are alive.
Let me make you my seal driver.

I could captain you if you'd crew for me
follow white flecked spindrift – float on a moonkissed sea.

Could you fancy me as a pirate bold,
or a longship Viking warrior with the old gods on
his side?
Well I'm an inshore man and I'm nobody's hero,
but I'll make you tight for a windy night and a dark
ride.
Let me take you in hand and bring you alive.
Going to make you my seal driver.

Cheerio

Along the coast road, by the headland
the early lights of winter glow.
I'll pour a cup to you my darling.
Raise it up – say Cheerio.

IAN ANDERSON : WALK INTO LIGHT

November 1983

Fly By Night
Made In England
Walk Into Light
Trains
End Game
Black & White Television
Toad In The Hole
Looking For Eden
User-Friendly
Different Germany

Fly By Night

It's hard to say I'm sorry.
May we just forget about today.
You see, I fly by night.
I fly by night.

I laid my love beside the door
and left you sleeping on the floor.
So long. I fly by night,
I fly by night.

And though you might think it's too bad of me
I have to leave you with used memories.

I have no stomach for the dawn.
I feel I should be moving on
and so I fly by night.

Now lady luck's deserted me.
The ghosts of love stand clear to see.
They also fly by night.

Strange figures in the dark.
Did Cupid strike and leave his mark?
It seems his arrows fly by night.
They fly by night.
Let's fly.

Made In England

Somewhere in a town in England
lay a babe with a curious smile.
He was of your father's children.
Born each side of a dry-stone mile.

He grew up through the schools and factories,
Brunel's[1] tunnels and bridges bold.
Grey towers built high on that Kingdom
with apartments still unsold.

Somewhere in a town in England.
Could be Newcastle, Leeds or Birmingham.
And were you made in
England's green and pleasant land?

He accepts no unemployment
and is to indeterminate station bred.
Is possessed of skills and reason.
Flies the flag upon his head.

Watches the democratic process
grind its way through the Commons cold,
filled with fiery infiltrators
who would pave the streets with England's gold.

1 Isambard Kingdom Brunel (1806 - 1859): builder of bridges, railways, metal ships

Walk Into Light

Close in, move out to where you want to go.
There's a crowd out there handclapping slow.
We're all powered up, switched on, the rig is tight.
Step into joy. Walk into light.
Never mind what some people say.
They're going to love you anyway.

Shake off that nervous twitch and feel your strength.
Stand astride the width and walk the length.
Those super-troopers fired and burning bright.
Step into joy. Walk into light.
Stand tall and be yourself.
You can do it for your health.

Maybe a circus ring, a disco floor.
Do like we do. And do some more.
A crowded office or a party night.
Step into joy. Walk into light.

Trains

Here I am at the end of the day
with a cup of cold coffee
from the station buffet.
On trains, on trains I seem
to spend my life on trains.

See the blue suit banker in the ticket line.
Got an Evening Standard with Playboy
hidden behind.
On trains, on trains he seems
to spend his life on trains.

Time after time.
Was I just dreaming?
Did I help you aboard?
Full passenger service –
let me help with the door.
Sit down take the weight off your feet.
Caught a train full of people I'd like
you to meet.
On trains, on trains we love
to spend our lives on trains.

Join the secret world of trains.
Feel the pleasure. Touch the pain.
Drift into yesterday.

Once and again
I was just thinking.
We could meet sometime
on the 17.30 where
I usually find
my friends at the end of the day.
May we pay your fare, lady?
We should like you to stay
on our train. On trains –
you'll have to spend your life
on trains.

I hear there's an office party on the 18.05.
You'll be home for Christmas if they
take you alive from the train.
Those trains, we have to spend our lives
on trains.

Once and again
I was just thinking.
We could meet any time
on number two platform
where I usually find
my friends at the end of the day.
On trains, trains, trains.

End Game

I'm slipping into grey.
And I was (in my way) good to you.
And you were good for me.
Bye bye my love.
Going to play the end game.

It's growing kind of still.
You know there always will be a dream
waiting for you when
sleep comes around.
I had to play the end game.

Bless us all. I must say,
it was good, you know.
Keep me in mind for
a re-match in warm snow.

The faces at the door
couldn't have looked more lost to see
me waving as I brush
away a tear.
Gone to play the end game.

Black And White Television

I looked in the mirror then
saw my face in a dream.
With eyes sharp as diamonds,
blessed with clear vision.
Things were not as they seemed.
Black and white television
stared back from the wall.
Is that my life?
Am I here at all?

Down in the High Road, see
motor cavalcades glide
past shopwindow dressers
desperately covering
all the parts they can hide.
Black and white television
stares at me again.
Is that their lives?
Even dummies pretend.

The truth is so hard to deny.
The answer is here.
The screen never lies.

Black and white television.
It's the right television.
Show me it's all a dream tonight.

The boys on the corner sulk
in their Suzuki haze.
In primary colours
(each year more startling)
but they still fade to grey
on black and white television.
It's sweeping the land.
Is that your life?
Do you understand?

The truth is so hard to deny.
The answer is here.
The screen never lies.

Black and white television.
Back the right television.
Black and white television.
Hard to fight television.
Show me it's all a dream tonight.

Toad In The Hole

I walk along the Strand
to catch the late ride home.
Shuttle through the evening gloom
knowing I forgot to phone.
The back door's open.
There's a chill blowing in.
Take your warm hands off me.
Let the night begin.
Shush your mouth.
Listen to me.
I won't say nothing –
just let me be your
toad in the hole.

Kicking through the wet leaves lying
all along the Station Road.
Past tired graffitti wailing,
raw emotion to unload.
There's coal in the fireplace
and money in the bank too.
Deep-pile carpets, tinsel wallpaper.
Still got the back room to do.
Don't be late.
Got a day's work behind me.
Feel a little devastated
but my nights are assigned to you.

Toad in the hole.

No tom-cat creeping, now
could ever be so bold
to hang around our place tonight
when I come in from the cold.
There's a straight-six in the garage
and some fine wine to cool.
Labour-savers in the kitchen,
room in the garden for a pool.

Shush your mouth.
Let imagination run
here in bed-sit heaven
where all the best wishing's done
to warm toad in the hole.

Looking For Eden

As I drove down the road to look for Eden
saw two young girls but left them standing there.
They were too late to get home on the underground
and probably too drunk, too drunk to care.

Can anyone tell me the way to Eden?
I'll ask them there, have they a job for me.
I'm not a fussy man, I can weed and hoe.
I'll be her Adam, she can be my Eve.

And where on earth are all those songs of Eden.
The fairy tales, the shepherds and wise men.
Just one old dosser lurching down Oxford Street
to spend his Christmas lying in the rain.

Don't anybody know the way to Eden.
I'm tired of living my life in free-fall.
They say it's somewhere out on the edge of town.
Perhaps it isn't really there at all.

Looking for Eden.

User-Friendly

Do we inhabit some micro-space
and interface through wires.
Dance on a printed circuit board
throw the software to the fires.
My memory's slim – so volatile
but I'm learning.
Plug yourself in. Stay for a while.
Un-discerning.

And on dusty terminals
finger me lightly do.
And QWERTY is the name of love
printed on the V.D.U.
Cut yourself free. We're all alone
communicating.
Don't bother me with arithmetic –
I'm waiting.

User-friendly.
That's what I am to you.

I have to break out of here.
Trapped in my hardware cell.
And come to you as you sleep tonight,
take you back into my hell.
Binary joys and digital sighs
so appealing.
I'm one of the boys and it's only
your mind that I'm stealing.
User-friendly.
That's all I am to you.

Different Germany

The lights are down in Germany
and Germany is closed to me
different somehow this time.

The airport's stiff, cold corridors
ring empty beats through hollow feet
that I find to be mine.

Different Germany.
History repeats somehow.
Different Germany.
Afraid to know you now.

And past my eyes with leathered gaze
stare clean-cut boys all dressed as men
in sharpened uniform.
Who turned the clock? (Moved on or back)
And what dark chill is gathering still
before the storm.

Out in the street a tableau double-glazed
with laughing girls whose fastened smiles
are clearly not meant for me.

UNDER WRAPS

September 1984

Lap Of Luxury
Under Wraps
European Legacy
Later, That Same Evening
Saboteur
Radio Free Moscow
Astronomy
Tundra
Nobody's Car
Heat
Paparazzi
Apogee
Automotive Engineering
General Crossing

Lap Of Luxury

The money won't last forever —
    rent man called twice today.
I hope some day you'll find me
    in the lap of luxury.

Searched for a new appartment
    but they don't grow on trees.
Just want to lay my head
    in the lap of luxury.

Stepped out on a new horizon —
    felt a new spring in my feet.
Found a job, it could set me up
    dangling in the lap of luxury.

And the gaffer is a man of substance —
    drives a jag and takes high tea.
Lives beyond the industrial wasteland,
    laughing in the lap of luxury.

I need money, now, to soothe my heart!

Buy me a Datsun or Toyota —
    get the tax man to agree
    all expenses I can muster
    from the lap of luxury.

Under Wraps

Keep it quiet. (Go slow.)
Circulate. Need to know.
Stamp the date upon your file –
    masquerade, but well worth while.

Wrapped in the warmth of you –
    wrapped up in your smile.
Wrapped in the folds of your attention.

Wear an air – (keep mum)
    of casual indifference.
Careful how you go
    about your usual business.

Wrapped in daydreams of you –
    wrapped up by your eyes.
Wrapped in the folds of your attention.
Under wraps! I've got you under wraps.

Tell you when – (not yet)
    soon the great unveiling.
Bless my boots! Upon my soul!
Secrecy, it is my failing.

Wrapped in your Summer night –
    wrapped in your Autumn leaves.
Wrapped in the Winter of your sleeping.

European Legacy

She smiles at me
   from beyond the eastern sea-shore.
Flashing jewelled eyes,
   she hoists her skirts so high.
Nouvelle cuisine or an oyster bar –
   it's really up to her.
I'll write every cheque she brings to me.
I shoot on sight –
   it's my European legacy.

Round the castle walls –
   about the Highlands and the Islands
   the faint reminders stand.
Visitors who took a hand
   a thousand years ago, or so –
   stranded high and dry by tides –
   washed up a new identity.
The channel's wide –
   but it's their European legacy.

I strain my eyes
   against the southern light advancing.
On whiter cliffs I'm high.
The sea birds roll and tumble as they fly.
I hear distant mainland music echo
   in my island ears.
My feet begin to move instinctively
   to the warmer beat of my European legacy.

She smiles at me
   from beyond the eastern sea-shore.
Flashing jewelled eyes,
   she hoists her skirts so high.
Nouvelle cuisine or an oyster bar –
   it's really up to her.
I'll write every cheque she brings to me.
She shoots on sight –
   it's her European legacy.

Later, That Same Evening

Later, that same evening, she ran.
I think she ran alone.
Later, she had early warning from
    a hidden phone.
Checked with the embassy –
    she might have been
    a million miles away.
Should I circulate her likeness
    at all airports without delay?
It was later –
    later that same evening.

Earlier, we had had a drink or four
    in some Kensington hotel.
Hard – it was hard to keep my mind
    on what she had to sell.
And with all business done
    we took a cab –
    should it be her place or mine?
Good security prevailed
    and I was home just after nine.
It was later –
    later that same evening.

Now I want you back.
Yes, they want you back.
We want you back.
My country wants you back.

Later, in the wee small hours,
    there was heavy traffic on the radio.
Scare at a channel port –
    small craft warnings to keep to shore.
Lobstermen thought they saw
    a submarine
    half submerged suspiciously.
Though I arrived too late,
    I'm sure she blew a kiss to me
    as the sub sailed out to sea.

Saboteur

In and out of shady places –
    walking on cold corners of the maze.
Following the trace you leave unwittingly.
I wanna be no Saboteur.
Oh, no, me no Saboteur.

Painted ducks across your landscape –
    happy in your domesticity (it don't come free).
Misfortune, like a Sparrow Hawk, hangs over you.
Wanna be no Saboteur.
No, no, me no Saboteur.

Deepest regrets I humbly offer you
    as I cut into your life.
With clean precision, all is simplified –
    pass the hat and pass the knife.

By now you must be worried, wondering
    who is me and what lies behind my art.
I'm only removing broken sea-shells from the beach –
    oh, no, me no Saboteur.

There's at least one of me inside your ranks
    in your factory or school.
I anticipate a cleansing opportunity
    to take the horns by the bull.

History forever writing
    pages to be cut or painted grey,
    or celebrated like Jesus in his
    temple rage
    as he chased the money-men away.

I wanna be no Saboteur.
Be no, be no Saboteur.

Radio Free Moscow

Tune into messages
    from the Eastern avenue.
Lock on to the ether –
    squeeze the signal through and through.
War of the air-waves
    making scare-waves.
I'm getting pictures
    from my radio (Free Moscow).
Moscow Radio.

Voice of America –
    symbol of the free.
Mine of disinformation
    pleading sympathy.
Down in the cold-war games
    forever naming names.
I'm getting pictures
    from my radio (Free Moscow).
Keep getting pictures
    from my radio (Free Moscow).

I put my headphones on –
    reach out on the beam.
Shutter up the windows –
    I'm getting up some steam.
Somebody's at the door
    catching me in the act –
    they've been keeping the score.
I'm getting pictures
    from my radio (Free Moscow).
Yes, I'm getting pictures
    from my radio (Free Moscow).

Astronomy

The middle lane has trapped my car
   in red-light claustrophobia.
I slip the shackles, cut the rope –
   stand naked with a telescope
   as the cat walks alone
   under a big sky.
Against the dark so thin and white –
   gonna be a big sky night.

Miss Galileo, come with me
   and view the new astronomy.
Black hole dressing on salad plate –
   quasar at the kissing gate.
Now the cat, he walks alone
   under a big sky.
Umbrella dome pin-pricked in lights –
   gonna be a big sky night.

My spectacles, my white lab coat –
   my coffee, thermos and my notes.
I pat my pockets. I got the keys
   to the secrets of the observatory.
And closing the door,
   I feel a new dawn
   as the darker sides align –
   you to yours and me to mine.

And now you stand, assisting me –
   I can touch what I can see, see, see.
I look in wonder, I feel no shame –
   see the consequences of the game.
Expand the universe.
Head for the Big Bang.
Reach for my switch and shout –
   gonna turn the big sky out.

There's got to be astronomy.
Astronomy.

Tundra

Short Arctic desert day –
    and someone left their snow-shoes in the tundra.
Look around every which way
    but I can't see just where the footprints go.
Is it a casual disappearance? –
    Plucked from the middle atmosphere
    like straw wind-blown.
No speck on the horizon –
    no simple message scrawled
    upon the snow.

Unearthly visitation –
    someone left their snow-shoes in the tundra.
Hungry buzzard flier
    circling round and round
    rattling death's tambourine.

Have to run it down the cold wire –
    late insertion in tomorrow's lost and found.
Should I spread out searching?
    But I'm a little thin upon the ground.

So I raise my lips to coax
    the last drop of brandy from the bottle.
Rest my feet and contemplate
    the mystery that's haunting
    this Siberian space.

Snow-shoes they bind me down –
    I'm just one more parasite of the surface layer.
I begin to get the feeling
    I've been on this stage before
    and I'm the only player.

One more Arctic desert day –
    another set of shoes out in the tundra snow.
make my fade to white-out
    and you can't see where my footprints go.

Nobody's Car

Black Volga following me –
 Nobody's car.
Mr. No-one at the wheel of
 Nobody's car.
Wet pavements, thin apartments –
 quiet dissent from darkened doorways.
I want out alive.
Speak up for me if you can.
So, careful how you drive
 in tourist city.

Slap in front of my hotel –
it's Nobody's car.
Is that my limousine?
No, it's Nobody's car.
Are you on routine assignment?
Plastic shades on black-browed eye-hole.
I read this book before.
I even saw the film.
How did the ending go?
 (Intourist city[1].)

Black out.

It's a weird scenario.
 I've seen a thousand times before
 but only on my video.

Feel my steps quick in the headlights
 of Nobody's car.
Down cobbled alley with no exit from
 Nobody's car.
Doors slam, two figures silhouette –
 somewhere before, I feel we've met.
Can't tell you any more.
I agreed to go along with all they asked of me.
Intourist city.
I drive Nobody's car.

1 Intourist: the official Russian tourist bureau

Heat

When the rats are running
    and the boys are gunning
    for heads on a tin plate –
    you can hear the footfall
    softly in the back yard.
And the black jack is called
    face up on the last card.

You'd better call your witness
    in your dirty business.
Trop tard sera le cri[1].
Better run while you can –
    better set the tall sail.
Better make the deep cover
    before the boys have you nailed.

There's just one chance to get away –
    I'll catch up with you another day.
I'll close my eyes and count to ten
    and come right after you again.

Grab your credit cards –
    cash in on your resources.
Take your passport from the drawer,
    don't stop to change the horses.

Get out of the heat.

Now can you feel the pressure?
Have you got the measure
    of being a wanted man?
Cold drink in your hand –
    hot sweat on your brow.
And there's no understanding
    going to help you now.

Trop tard sera le cri: quote out of a French school book of Ian Anderson's; *Too late will be the cry / when the ice-cream salesman has gone by*

Grab your credit cards –
    cash in on your resources.
Take your passport from the drawer,
    don't stop to change the horses.
Notify all parties
    of an earlier vacation.
No use trying to board the train
    after it's left the station.

Get out of the heat.

Paparazzi

Paparazzi, can't make the man.
Paparazzi, can't break the man.

Next to the transit lounge
    see the Paparazzi tears.
No-one came in today
    from Boston or Tangiers.
And in departures –
    only faceless trippers trip,
    loaded with duty free
    held in white knuckle grip.

Snap it up, flash away –
    steal a camel for a day.
Break the story in heavy type –
    the news is running late tonight.

Be-decked with Nikon necklaces
    hear the Paparazzi cries.
Under their noses walk
    the famous in disguise.
Conspicuously huddled there
    but no-one stops to look.
They've got their crayons out
    to colour in the book.

Snap it up, flash away –
    steal a camel for a day.
Break the story in heavy type –
    Paparazzi won't be home tonight.

Paparazzi – write it down.
Paparazzi – turn it round.
Paparazzi – turn it, fake it,
    break it.
    'Cos it's a story.
Now someone's cut the lines
    communication's down.
All photo film is fogged.
Celebrities surround
    and jab their fingers at me.
They kiss but I can't tell.
Even poor Paparazzi
    must have privacy as well.

Snap it up, flash away –
    steal a camel for a day.
Break the story in heavy type –
    the news is running late tonight.

Snap it up, flash away –
    steal a camel for a day.
Break the story in heavy type –
    Paparazzi won't be home tonight.

Apogee

Sailing round the true-blue sphere –
    is it too late to bale out of here?
Well, there has to be some better way
    to turn back the night,
    spin on to yesterday.

The old man and his crew –
    after all these years,
    it's apogee[1].
Pilot training and remorse –
    spirit friends fly too,
    at apogee.
Apogee – solar bright.
Apogee – through the night.
Apogee – overground.
Don't think I'll be coming down.

Screened for a stable mate
    with nerves of ice we flew,
    at apogee.
No creativity allowed
    to pass through stainless veins of steel,
    at apogee.
Apogee – put the kettle on.
Tight-lipped – soldier on.
High point – communicate.
Don't forget to urinate.

So glad they put this window in.
How to explain, how to begin?
See! Tennyson and Wordsworth[2] there
    waiting for me in the cold, thin air.

1 Apogee: the point in an orbit furthest away from the earth
2 Lord Alfred Tennyson (1809 - 1892), William Wordsworth (1770 - 1850): English poets of the Romanti
  school

Beware a host of unearthly daffodils
    drifting golden, turned up loud.
Tell the boys back home,
    I'm gonna get some.

The Wrong Stuff's loose in here –
    I'm climbing up the walls,
    at apogee.
So hoist the skull and bones –
    death and glory's free,
    at apogee.

A stranger wind, a solar breeze –
    I'm walking out upon the starry seas.
See pyramids, see standing stones –
    pink cotton undies and blue telephones.

Goodbye, cruel world that was my home –
    there's a cleaner space out there to roam.
Put my feet up on the moons of Mars –
    sit back, relax and count the stars.

Automotive Engineering

In the hands of science –
    the complete appliance.
We're moved to motor.
Do you fly a Spitfire?
Do you slide on a tea-tray?
Or walk on a short trip (Sundays).
Or drive come what may (enjoy).

Automotive science and engineering.

When big was better –
    and fast was chic,
    the oil was cheaper –
    now we're up the creek.
But the Japs are coming
    and everyone's turbo'd
    and carbon fibre
    is the way to go, go.

Down at the robot factory
    things are humming.
New radical suspension –
    no humans testing.
(Wind it up, wind it up.)
Take a trip
    in your Freudian slip.
Doctor Ferdinand (Ferdie)
    has you in his grip.

General Crossing

It's an old profession
    of subtle artillery.
Rough wheels meshing –
    button out, button in.

The tall General will mine
    a few bridges tonight,
    stroking soft machinery.
Fanfare at dawn
    courting green steel
    lined up for World War One
    (Two, Three, Four).

It's an old profession
    of subtle artillery.
Rough wheels meshing –
    on a landscape with no trees.

The tall General points
    to the distance –
    disconnects his power supply.
Writes a stiff note to his nearest
    and dearest –
    he takes the battle plan
    and contemplates his fly.

The tall General
    flies by the seat of history.
The tall General
    is crossing.
The tall General
    he thinks inevitability.
The tall General
    is definitely crossing.
With spit and with polish –
    time for desperate measures.

The pain in the forehead
   from holding up to the pressures
   of life on the rim
   of the convenient alliance.
Out on the rim –
   let me out on the rim.

The tall General will walk
   across the compound
   with his briefcase and I.D.
Later they'll post him
   seemingly missing –
   he's gone to be a Generalski.

CREST OF A KNAVE

September 1987

Steel Monkey
Farm On The Freeway
Jumpstart
Said She Was A Dancer
Dogs In The Midwinter
Budapest
Mountain Men
The Waking Edge
Raising Steam

Steel Monkey

As the moon slips up, and the sun sets down,
I'm a highrise jockey, and I'm heaven-bound.
Do the workboot shuffle, loose brains from brawn.
I'm a monkey puzzle and the lid is on.

Can you guess my name? Can you guess my trade?
I'm going to catch you anyway.
You might be right. I'll give you guesses three.
Feel me climbing up your knee.

Guess what I am. I'm a steel monkey.

Now some men hustle and some just think.
And some go running before you blink.
Some look up and some look down
from three hundred feet above the ground.

Can you guess my name? And can you guess my trade?
Well, I won't rest before the world is made.
Arm in arm the angels fly.
Keep me from falling out the sky.

Steel monkey.

I work in the thunder and I work in the rain.
I work at my drinking, and I feel no pain.
I work on women, if they want me to.
You can have me climb all over you.

Now, have you guessed my name?
And have you guessed my trade?
I'm cheap at the money I get paid.
In the sulphur city, where men are men,
we bolt those beams then climb again.

Steel monkey.

Farm On The Freeway

Nine miles of two-strand topped with barbed wire
laid by the father for the son.
Good shelter down there on the valley floor,
down by where the sweet stream runs.
Now they might give me compensation …
That's not what I'm chasing. I was a rich man before yesterday.
Now, all I have got is a cheque and a pickup truck.
I left my farm on the freeway.

They're busy building airports on the south side …
Silicon chip factory on the east.
And the big road's pushing through along the valley floor.
Hot machine pouring six lanes at the very least.
Now, they say they gave me compensation …
That's not what I'm chasing. I was a rich man before yesterday.
Now all I have left is a broken-down pickup truck.
Looks like my farm is a freeway.

They forgot they told us what this old land was for.
Grow two tons the acre, boy, between the stones.
This was no Southfork, it was no Ponderosa.
But it was the place that I called home.
They say they gave me compensation …
That's not what I'm chasing. I was a rich man before yesterday.
And what do I want with a million dollars and a pickup truck?
When I left my farm under the freeway.

Jump Start

In the dark of the city backwoods, something stirs then slips away.
Law and order in darkest Knightsbridge. Crime and punishment at play.
Hey, Mr. Policeman, won't you come on over. Hook me up to the power lines
of your love.
Jump start, or tow me away.

And through the bruised machinery, the smoking haze of industry.
Another day with ball and chain. I do my time, then home again.
Hey, Mrs. Maggie, won't you come on over. Hook me up to the power lines
of your love.
Jump start, or tow me away.

Well, should I blame the officers? Or maybe, I should blame the priest?
Or should I blame the poor foot soldier
who's left to make the most from least?
Hey, Jack Ripper, won't you come on over. Hook me up to the power lines
of your love.
Jump start, or tow me away.

You can blame the newsman talking at you on the satellite TV
And if you're fighting for your shipyards you might as well just blame the sea.
Hey, Mr. Weatherman, come on over. Hook me up to the power lines
of your love.
Jump start, or tow me away.

Said She Was A Dancer

She said she was a dancer. If I believed it, it was my business.
She surely knew a thing or two about control.
Next to the bar we hit the samovar. She almost slipped right through my fingers.
It was snowing outside and in her soul.

Well, maybe you're a dancer, and maybe I'm the King of Old Siam.
I thought it through … best to let the illusion roll.
I wouldn't say I've never heard that tale before,
my frozen little señorita,
but if your dream is good, why not share it when the nights are cold?

Hey Moscow, what's your story? Lady, take your time, don't hurry.
Maybe a student of the agricultural plan.
Hey Moscow, what's your name? If you don't want to say, don't worry.
It would probably be hard for me to make it scan.

With her phrase book in her silk soft hand
she spoke in riddles while the vodka listened.
I said, »Let me look up love, if I might be so bold.«
She was the nearest thing to Rock and Roll
that side of the velvet curtain
that separates eastern steel from western gold.

Hey Miss Moscow, what's your story?
You needn't speak aloud, just whisper.
Am I just the closest thing to an Englishman?
You've seen me in your magazines, or maybe on state television.
I'm your Pepsi-Cola, but you won't take me out the can.
She said she was a dancer – so she did.

She said she was a dancer. If I believed it, it was my business.
It felt like a merry dance that I was being led.
So I stole one kiss. It was a near miss.
She looked at me like I was Jack the Ripper.
She leaned in close. »Goodnight,« was all she said.
So I took myself off to bed.

Dogs In The Midwinter

You ever had a day like I had today,
when things are stacked up bad?
You look around and every face you see
seems guaranteed to send you mad.
And you peer into those hallowed institutions.
And they bark at you from every side.
But the bite goes wide.

I see them running with their tails hanging low
like dogs in the midwinter.
The prophets and the wise men and the hard politicos
are all dogs in the midwinter.
Let the breath from the mountain still the pain,
clear water from the fountain run sweeter than the rain.
Dogs in the midwinter.

The boss man and the tax man and the moneylenders growl …
like dogs in the midwinter.
The weaker of the herd can feel their eyes and hear them howl
like dogs in the midwinter.
Though the fox and the rabbit are at peace,
cold doggies in the manger turn last suppers into feasts.
Dogs in the midwinter.

You ever had a day like I had today –
dogs in the midwinter.
You look around and every face you see –
dogs in the midwinter.
And you peer into those hallowed institutions.
And they bark at you from every side.
But the bite goes wide.

We're all running on a tightrope, wearing slippers in the snow …
we're all dogs in the midwinter.
The ice is ever thinner. Be careful how you go
like dogs in the midwinter.
And it's hard to find true equilibrium
when you're looking at each other down the muzzle of a gun.
Dogs in the midwinter.

Budapest

I think she was a middle-distance runner …
(the translation wasn't clear).
Could be a budding stately hero.
International competition in a year.
She was a good enough reason for a party …
(well, you couldn't keep up on a hard track mile)
while she ran a perfect circle.
And she wore a perfect smile
in Budapest … hot night in Budapest.

We had to cozzy up in the old gymnasium …
dusting off the mandolins and checking on the gear.
She was helping out at the back-stage …
stopping hearts and chilling beer.
Yes, and her legs went on forever.
Like staring up at infinity
through a wisp of cotton panty
along a skin of satin sea.
Hot night in Budapest.

You could cut the heat, peel it back with the wrong side of a knife.
Feel it blowing from the sidefills. Feel like you were playing for your life
(if not the money).
Hot night in Budapest.

She bent down to load the ice box
and stuffed some more warm white wine in
like some weird unearthly vision
wearing only T-shirt, pants and skin.
You know, it rippled, just a hint of muscle.
But the boys and me were heading west
so we left her to the late crew
and a hot night in Budapest.
It was a hot night in Budapest.

She didn't speak much English language …
(she didn't speak much anyway).
She wouldn't make love, but she could make a good sandwich
and she poured sweet wine before we played.

Hey, Budapest, cha, cha, cha. Let's watch her now.

I thought I saw her at the late night restaurant.
She would have sent blue shivers down the wall.
But she didn't grace our table.
In fact, she wasn't there at all.
Yes, and her legs went on forever.
Like staring up at infinity.
Her heart was spinning to the west-lands
and she didn't care to be
that night in Budapest.
Hot night in Budapest.

Mountain Men

The poacher and his daughter
throw soft shadows on the water in the night.
A thin moon slips behind them
as they pull the net with no betraying light.
And later on the coast road, I meet them
and the old man winks a smile.
And who am I to fast deny the right
to take a fish once in a while?
I walk with them, they wish me luck
when I ship out on the Sunday from the kyle.
And from the church I hear them singing
as the ship moves sadly from the pier.
Oh, poacher's daughter, Sunday best,
two hundred brave souls share the farewell tear.

There's a house on the hillside, where the drifting sands are born.
Lay down and let the slow tide wash me
back to the land where I came from.
Where the mountain men are kings
and the sound of the piper counts for everything.

Did my tour, did my duty. I did all they asked of me.
Died in the trenches and at Alamein[1]
… died in the Falklands[2] on TV.
Going back to the mountain kings
where the sound of the piper counts for everything.

Long generations from the Isles
sent to tread the foreign miles
where the spiral ages meet.
Felt naked dust beneath their feet.
Future sun called winds to blow
and the past and present hard-eyed crow
flew hunting high and circling low over blackened plains of Eden.

---

[1] El-Alamein: coastal town in Egypt, west of Alexandria; the battles of El-Alamein (30.6. - 3.11.1942) stopped Rommel's advance on Alexandria and enabled the British under Montgomery to mount a counter offensive.
[2] The Falklands: Falkland war between Britain and Argentina, 1982

There's a child and a woman praying for an end to the mystery.
Hoping for a word in a letter
fair wind-blown from across the sea
to where the mountain men are kings
and the sound of the piper counts for everything.

There's a house on the hillside, where the drifting sands are born.
Lay down and let the slow tide wash me
back to the land where I came from.
Where the mountain men are kings
and the sound of the piper counts for everything.
Where the real mountain men are kings
and the sound of that piper counts for everything.

Feel the naked dust beneath my toes
while the future sun calls winds to blow
and the past and present black-eyed crow
flies hunting high and circling low
between dream mountains of our Eden.

The Waking Edge

As I wake up in a room somewhere …
dawn light not yet showing.
There's just a thin horizon between me and her …
the edge of a half-dream glowing.

Well, you know, I felt her in my dream last night.
Strange how the sheets are warm beside me.
Now, how do I catch the waking edge?
As it slips to the far and wide of me.

Didn't I try to hold it down?
Freeze on the picture, hang sharp on the sound.
Catch the waking edge
another time.

Familiar shadows in my hotel room
are still here for the taking.
They seem to linger on as the street lights fade
and the empty dawn is breaking.

Private movie showing in my head …
what button do I press for re-run?
And how do I catch the waking edge?
The edge of a dream about someone.

Well, you know, I felt her in my dream last night …
now the sheets are cold beside me.

Raising Steam

Over high plains, through the snow …
roll those tracks out, don't you know
I'm raising steam.
Thin vein creeping; hot blood flow …
spill a little where the new towns grow.
I got my whole life hanging in a sack,
heading out into that wide world wide.
You got your locomotive sitting on your track
and I don't care which way I ride.
I may not be coming back.

Left a lady with a heart
all in pieces come apart
raising steam.
That engine up front must
have a heart big enough for the both of us.
Riding shotgun on the sunset, stare it in the eye,
rocking on my heels out to the west.
Funny how the whole world, historically,
feels the urge to chase the sun to rest.
We may not be coming back.

Let me be your engineer …
have you smiling ear to ear
raising steam.
And will you tell me how it feels
when you're up and rolling on your driving wheels?
I got my whole life hanging in a sack,
heading out into that wide world wide.
I'll be your locomotive blowing off its stack
and I don't care which way I ride.
I may not be coming back.
Raising steam.

20 YEARS OF JETHRO TULL

July 1988

I. THE RADIO ARCHIVES AND RARE TRACKS

Song For Jeffrey (*This Was*)
Love Story (*Living In The Past*)
Fat Man (*Stand Up*)
Bourrée (*Stand Up*)
Stormy Monday Blues (Eckstine / Crowder / Hines)
A New Day Yesterday (*Stand Up*)
Cold Wind To Valhalla (*Minstrel In The Gallery*)
Minstrel In The Gallery (*Minstrel In The Gallery*)
Velvet Green (*Songs From The Wood*)
Grace (*Minstrel In The Gallery*)
Jack Frost And The Hooded Crow
I'm Your Gun
Down At The End Of Your Road
Coronach (Words and music by David Palmer)
Summerday Sands
Too Many Too
March The Mad Scientist
Pan Dance (Instrumental)
Strip Cartoon
King Henry's Madrigal (Instrumental / trad., arr. David Palmer)
A Stitch In Time
17
One For John Gee (Instrumental / Michael Abrahams)
Aeroplane
Sunshine Day (Words and music by Michael Abrahams)

Jack Frost And The Hooded Crow

Through long December nights we talk in words of rain or snow
while you, through chattering teeth, reply and curse us as you go.
Why not spare a thought this day for those who have no flame
to warm their bones at Christmas time?
Say Jack Frost and the Hooded Crow.

Now, as the last broad oak leaf falls, we beg: consider this –
there's some who have no coin to save for turkey, wine or gifts.
No children's laughter round the fire, no family left to know.
So lend a warm and a helping hand –
say Jack Frost and the Hooded Crow.

As holly pricks and ivy clings,
your fate is none too clear.
The Lord may find you wanting, let your good fortune disappear.
All homely comforts blown away and all that's left to show
is to share your joy at Christmas time
with Jack Frost and the Hooded Crow.

I'm Your Gun

Blew my smoke on a sunny day
when the first black powder came my way.
Hot lead ball from a muzzle cold –
to win fair lady and take your gold.
I know it hardly seems the time –
(I am your gun)
to talk of blue steel so sublime.
I can understand your point of view.
To tell the truth, I scare me too.

Match, wheel and flintlock, they all caught your eye.
Pearl-handled ladies' models, scaled down to size.
I am the peacemaker, so the theory goes.
But I don't choose the company I keep –
and it shows.

I am your gun.
Love me, I'm your gun.

Maxim and Browning, they helped me along.
Stoner, Kalashnikov[1] – thrilled to my song.
Now one of me exists, for each one of you.
So how can you blame me for the things that I do?

Now I take second place to the motor car
in the score of killing kept thus far.
And just remember, if you don't mind –
it's not the gun that kills
but the man behind.

I am your gun.

1 Maxim, Browning, Stoner, Kalashnikoff: inventors of small arms

Down At The End Of Your Road

I am your neighbour, I seem most respectable.
But underneath I'm an iniquitous toad.
So many dreadful mishaps have befallen you –
down at the end of your road.
And I live down the end of your road.

I'm working on ways to remove you from paradise –
from your striped lawn and your new swimming pool.
I place broken bottles in your geraniums –
sabotage your gardening tools.
And I live down the end of your road.

By day I am a real estate agent gentleman.
I deal in fine properties – cheap at the price.
After dark, I plan my most devious practises
which you might think are not very nice.

Designing a system to reverse your plumbing –
welling up, as you sit on your private throne,
will come up all kinds of vile and despicable nasties
you would rather not have in your home.
And I live down the end of your road.

Dispensed loathsome creatures in your drawing room.
Sent doggy poo-poos in your morning mail.
Rats' heads and larks' wings should set your tums turning
and your houses will soon be for sale.
And I live down the end of your road.

I live down at the end of your road.

Coronach[1]

(Words and music by David Palmer)

Grey the mist – cold the dawn;
cruel the sea and stern the shore.
Brave the man who sets his course
for Albion[2].

Sweet the rose – sharp the thorn;
meek the soil and proud the corn.
Blessed the lamb that would be born
within this green and pleasant land.
Hi–O–Ran–I–O
Hi–O–Ran–I–O

Brown furrows shine
beneath the rain washed blue.
Bright crystal streams
from eagle mountains pour.
Fortune has smiled on those who wake anew,
within this fortress nature built
to stay the hand of war.

With the wind from the east
came the first of those who tread
upon this stone, this stone of kings;
this realm, this new Jerusalem.
Hi–O–Ran–I–O
Hi–O–Ran–I–O

1 Coronach: Scottish funeral song; recording produced by David Palmer for UK Channel 4 TV historical
   series *The Blood Of The British*, 1986
2 Albion: former name of Britain

Summerday Sands

I once met a girl with her life in her hands
and we lay together on the summerday sands.
I gave her my raincoat and told her, »Lady, be good!«
And we made truth together, where no one else would.

I smiled through her fingers and ran the dust through her hands –
the hour-glass of reason on the summerday sands.

We sat as the sea caught fire.
Waited as the flames grew higher
in her eyes.
We watched the eagle born –
wings clipped, tail feathers shorn
but we saw him rise –
over summerday sands.

Came the ten o'clock curfew.
She said, »I must start my car.
I'm staying with someone I met last night in a bar.«
I called from my wave top –
»At least tell me your name!«
She smiled from her wheelspin
and said, »It's all the same.«
I thought for a minute, jumped back on dry land –
left one set of footprints on the summerday sands.

I once met a girl with her life in her hands
and we lied together on the summerday sands.

Too Many Too

Too many drivers in too many cars.
Too many lost souls drinking in too many bars.
Too many heroes stepping on too many toes.
Too many yes-men nodding when they really mean no.
Too many lives each cat can lose –
we've got too many too.
Too many too.

Too much sunshine. Too many drops of rain.
Too many equal and average children who will all grow up the same.
Too many fireside politicians holding too many views.
Too many questions – but there are answers too few.
Too many lives each cat can lose –
we've got too many too.

If I were a liar – yes, and you were a cheat –
there would be too many places where we all could meet.
Too many temples where we could worship the beast.
Where he who thinks he has the most in fact has the least.
Too many lives each cat can lose –
I've got too many too.
I've got too many too.

March The Mad Scientist

What would you like for Christmas –
a new polarity?
You're binary, and desperate to deal
in higher figures
that lick us with their hotter flame –
lick each and everyone the same.
And March, the mad scientist,
rings a new change
in ever-dancing colours.

He rings it here and he rings it …
but no one stops to see
the change of fate and the fate of change
that slips into his pocket –
so he locks it all away from view
and shares not what he thought you knew.
And April is summer-bound.
And February's blue.
And no one stops to see the colours.

Strip Cartoon

Fish and chips, sandpaper lips and a rainy pavement.
Soho lights, another night – thinking of you.
Black cat, sat on the wall, winks at me darkly.
Suggesting ways and means that I might win a smile –

as you leave the place where you work until 12.30
and the policeman nods as you pass along his beat.
Sweaty feet, troubled brow – we're all in the same game, lady.
Life's no bowl of cherries – it's a black and white strip cartoon.

I've been warned that you and your friends are crazy
as from your hearts you bare your parts to the gentlemen
who, while they drool, trying to keep cool,
spill their Scotch and water.
But I'm not that way, I must say – I'd much prefer to see
you in your texturised rubber rainwear around 12.30.
Come and play shades of grey in my black and white strip cartoon.
Strip cartoon is all I'm after.
Strip cartoon is all I crave –
so come to my place around 12.30
'cos I'm a leading politician
at a dangerous age.

A Stitch In Time

I work in dark factories – a cog in the big wheel
driving grey satanic mills and weaving sad stories.
And faceless masters – oh, they pay me plenty –
crumbs from their luncheon packs, harsh wine from
bottles half empty.

A stitch in time saves nine.
Said Cock Robin from the wall.
It's an early bird catches the worm.
Show a little pride before you fall.
So I flew to the south sun with birds of a feather
to drink in the warm nights and tell of fine weather.
A stitch in time saves nine.

Listen all you young folk – your lives on a timetable
clocking on twenty-one – fly while you're able.
A stitch in time saves nine.

17

I remember when we had a lot of things to do –
impressed by all the words we read
and the heroes that we knew.
Climb on your dream – a dream of our own making
to find a place that we could later lose
to whatever time would bring.

We were seventeen and the cakeman was affecting you –
moving you to greater things (in a lesser way)
you had to prove.
The clock struck summertime. You were going round in circles now.
Wishing you were seventeen. At twenty-one, it was a long time gone.
And now here you are. You're locked in your own excuse.
The circle's getting smaller every day.
You're busy planning the next fifty years.
So stay the way you are and keep your head down to the same old ground.
Just paint your picture boy until you find
a closed circle's better than an open line.

Yes, stay the way you are. I got a circle that's the same as yours.
It may be bigger, but I've more to lose.
Who is the luckier man – me or you?

Aeroplane[1]

Flying – made of sticks and paper –
aeroplane.
Dying – is the wind but climbing –
my aeroplane.
Blowing and going somewhere high –
in the evening tumbling down –
but it's surely been up there.

Crying – want to live my life as
my aeroplane.

Sighing in the sun's eye, but softly –
my aeroplane.

Lonely, but only till it comes down
where there's people running round.
But it's surely been up there.

Flying – my aeroplane.

1 Aeroplane: original recording by the John Evan Band, 1967; published by MGM by mistake under the
name Jethro Toe

Sunshine Day

(Words and music by Mick Abrahams)

Woke up this morning to look at things with their funny way.
Why can't they be like they used to be only yesterday.
Ooh – bring back my sunshine day.

I look at things that once were mine with such despair.
Why do the things I say only fall on empty air?
Ooh – bring back my sunshine day.
My mind cries: Bring back my sunshine day.

I say the things I used to say, but they don't seem right.
Why does this world seem like the darkest endless night?
Ooh – bring back my sunshine day.
Bring back my sunshine day.

20 YEARS OF JETHRO TULL

II. FLAWED GEMS AND THE OTHER SIDE OF TULL

Lick Your Fingers Clean
The Chateau D'Isaster Tapes
a) Scenario
b) Audition
c) No Rehearsal
Beltane
Crossword
Saturation
Jack-A-Lynn
Motoreyes
Blues Instrumental (Untitled)
Rhythm In Gold
Part Of The Machine
Mayhem, Maybe
Overhang
Kelpie
Living In These Hard Times
Under Wraps 2 (*Under Wraps*)
Only Solitaire (*WarChild*)
Salamander (*Too Old To Rock'n'Roll …*)
Moths (*Heavy Horses*)
Nursie (*Living In The Past*)

Lick Your Fingers Clean

I'll see you at the weighing in
when your life's sum-total's made.
And you set your wealth in godly deeds
against the sins you've laid.
So place your final burden
on your hard-pressed next of kin:
Send the chamber pot back down the line
to be filled up again.
Take your mind off your election
and try to get it straight.
And don't pretend perfection –
you'll be crucified too late.
And he'll say you really should make the deal
as he offers round the hat.
Well, you'd better lick your fingers clean, I thank you all for that.
And as you join the good ship earth
and you mingle with the dust
be sure to leave your underpants
with someone you can trust.
And the hard-headed social worker who bathes his hands in blood
will welcome you with arms held high
and cover you with mud.
And he'll say you really should make the deal
as he offers round the hat.
Well, you'd better lick your fingers clean, I thank you all for that.

The Chateau D'Isaster Tapes

a) *Scenario*

In long years of ancient time, stood alone a friend of mine.
Reflected by the ever-burning sigh of a god who happened by.
And in the dawn, there came the song of some sweet lady singing in his ear.
Your god has gone, and from now on, you'll have to learn to hate
the things you fear.

We want to know, are we inside the womb
of passion plays, and by righteousness consumed?
Or just in lush contentment of our souls?

And so began the age of man.
They left his body in the sand.
Their glasses raised to a god on high
who smiled upon them from the sky.
So take the stage. Spin down the ages. Loose the passion.
Spill the rage upon your son who holds the gun up to your head –
the play's begun.

b) *Audition*

Then God, the director, smells a rat.
Pulls another rabbit from His hat.
Sniffs the air and He says »Well, that's that – I'm going.«
The actors milling helplessly – the script is blowing out to sea.
But what the hell, we didn't even pass an audition.
The lines you'll have to improvise. The words are written in
the eyes of politicians who despise their fathers.
And so the play necessitates that all you boys participate
in fierce competition to eliminate each other.

And groupies, on their way to war,
get to write the next film score.
But the rock and roll star knows his glory is really nothing.
Men of religion, on the make,
pledge an oath they undertake to
make you white for God's own sake, and none other.

While ladies get their bedding done
to win themselves a bouncing son –
but bad girls do it for the fun of just being.
And me, I'm here to sing along,
and I'm not concerned with righting wrongs,
just asking questions that belong without an answer.
But God is laughing up his sleeve
as He pours himself another cup of tea,
and He waves goodbye to you and me,
at least for now.

c) *No Rehearsal*

Did you learn your lines today? Well, there is no rehearsal.
The tickets have all been sold for tomorrow's matinee.
There's a telegram from the writer,
but there is no rehearsal.
The electrician has been told to make the spotlights brighter.
There's one seat in the circle – five hundred million in the stalls.
Simply everyone will be there, but the safety curtain falls when
the bomb that's in the dressing room
blows the windows from their frames.
And the prompter in his corner is sorry that he came.

Did you learn your lines today? Well there is no rehearsal.
The interval will last until the ice-cream lady melts away.
The twelve piece orchestra are here, but there is no rehearsal.
The first violinist's hands are chilled – he's gone deaf in both ears.
Well, the scenery is colourful, but the paint is so damn thin.
You see the wall behind is crumbling,
and the stage door is bricked-in.
But the audience keep arriving
'till they're standing in the wings.
And we take the final curtain call, and the ceiling crashes in.

Beltane

Have you ever stood in an April wood
and called the new year in?
While the phantoms of three thousand years fly
as the dead leaves spin.
There's a snap in the grass behind your feet
and a tap upon your shoulder.
And the thin wind crawls along your neck –
it's just the old gods getting older.
And the kestrel drops like a fall of shot and
the red cloud hanging high –
come – a Beltane[1].

Have you ever loved a lover of the old elastic truth?
And doted on the daughter in the ministry of youth?
Thrust your head between the breasts of the fertile innocent.
And taken up the cause of love, for the sake of argument.
Or while the kisses drop like a fall of shot
from soft lips in the rain –
come – a Beltane.

Happy old new year to you and yours.
The sun's up for one more day, to be sure.
Play it out gladly, for your card's marked again.

Have you walked around your parks and towns so knife-edged orderly?
While the fires are burned on the hills upturned
in far-off wild country.
And felt the chill on your window sill
as the green man[2] comes around.
With his walking cane of sweet hazel – brings it crashing down.
Sends your knuckles white as the thin stick bites.
Well, it's just your growing pains.
Come – a Beltane.

1 Beltane: refer to footnote in *Cup Of Wonder (Songs From The Wood)*
2 The green man: refer to footnote in *Jack-In-The-Green (Songs From The Wood)*

Crossword

Walking on air, shoulder and head above you.
Down in the street, black canyons walking through.
Hooded sad eyes, fixed on your shuffle shoes.
Life is a clue in your crossword.

Typewriter turk. Telephone terror takes time to wind down.
Push-button finger shakes.
City of dreams. Back to your quiet nightmare.
Your life is a clue in the crossword.

Working to rule in your own time.
Drag yourself home to your star sign page.
Staying awake on cold yesterday's steak and warm beer.

Ladder of string – climbing to sweet success.
Homework aside. Your brain on the train to test.
Pick up the news (you left on the seat beside you).
Your life is a clue in the crossword.

Saturation

They left me, leaving my house on fire, me running round –
got out through the window.
While clinging to the skirts of fate
was not my idea of fun
I jumped to it gladly.
The town was filled with smoke and hate.
Came to my senses just too late
to realise that all I ever owned
was borrowed. I thanked them for having shown
me that nothing ever really belongs to anyone.

They burned my books and they broke my car,
and they gave the dog to a man who used him for breeding.
They felled my trees and they trampled flowers and threw
the kitten into my new pool.
The same things done to other men had made them run away from the city.
This being the case, I joined them there and breathing air spent
the night with these new friends.

Jack-A-Lynn

Cold aeroplanes, slow boats, warm trains
remind me of Jack-A-Lynn.
Plush hotels and pretty girls
won't cheer the misty mood I'm in.
Silly, sad – I never had to write this before –
oh, Jack-A-Lynn.

Funny how long nights allow
thoughts of Jack-A-Lynn.
When phantoms tread around my bed
to offer restless dreams they bring.
And it's just the time and place to find
a sad song to play
for Jack-A-Lynn.

Magpies that shriek, old boots that leak
call me to Jack-A-Lynn.
Coal-black cats in policemen's hats
nosing where the mice have been.
And the long miaow's beginning now
and I'm far, far from home –
and Jack-A-Lynn.

Motoreyes

Out on the fast and free way,
humming along through a built-up ad-man's dream.
Streaking past in a cloud of spray
goes a high-performance motor queen.
And she looks round at me
reflecting neon in her motoreyes.
And now the chase is on.
I know who'll be the loser – me.

See the end curve coming, then we're
back on the street through the late theatre crowds.
And the stop lights go and we're cruising side by side
still humming loud.
And she looks round again –
her motoreyes going to tell me when.
Puts her right foot to the floor.
Shows me she's no slow woman.

She takes her cafe noir, smokes small cigars
showing just a touch of thigh (sigh!).
And sips her whisky straight, and she stays up late
to kiss the morning bye-bye.

Now we're out of town, going to shake her down
if I can stay along.
Got my blue light on, put her in the net
with my siren song.
Pulls over to the side –
her motoreyes are staring wide.
She flashes her I.D.
and makes a bigger fool of me.

Rhythm In Gold

I have to call you up. Think I've seen a vision of rhythm in gold.
No cat could ever move that way. No puss would dare to be so bold.
Must tell the boys to follow you.
Catch you where you go to ground.
A lady of means, I can see. Rhythm in gold is getting to me.
What's your name, and where can I find you?

Are you just a rich man's friend,
or was it always in the family?
You seem to throw the challenge down,
by the way you didn't even look at me.
Put the boys on you. Immobilise your nine-eleven.

There's nothing I could do for you that would really matter much anyway.
You belong to everyone. Rhythm in gold's the number that you play.
Put the boys on you. Sabotage your nine-eleven.

Part Of The Machine

Everybody's jumping on the circus train.
Some jump high, some jump off again.
And the razzmatazz is rolling, woman folk unveiled.
All truths to light, all crosses nailed.
Aiming high where the eagle circles –
where he keeps his tail feathers clean.
And wonders, »Am I still a free bird?
Or just a part of the machine.«

They hitch their covered wagons and they roll out west.
Politics in the pockets of their Sunday best.
Shaking hands, kissing babies, for all that they're worth.
Oh, they promise you gold, promise heaven on earth.

Still, that old bald eagle circles –
it's not the first time that he's seen
his reflection in the eyes of innocence.
He's become just another
part of the machine.

I wish I had an eagle like you –
to look up to.
He could be my wings to fly in a big bird sky
up above the whole machine.

Smart guys aren't running – they're home and dry.
Up in the mountains where the eagle flies.
They wouldn't take that job
offered on a plate.
They got to fly with the eagle, and he won't wait.
Looking down on the smoke and the factories
till the truth creeps up unseen.
They see themselves in the faces of their children
and realise they too are
part of the machine.

I wish I had an eagle like you –
to wake up to.
He could be my wings to fly
in a big bird sky, hey –
let's be part of the machine.
Part of the machine.

Mayhem, Maybe

When we're working nights, the village round
the old church becomes scary town.
All curtained windows and bolted doors
but never an eye to see
as us fairy folk sweep from the hill.
Never caught us and never will.
Pulling roses and daffodils —
mayhem in the high degree.

The blacksmith chased us all to ground.
They searched all night — we were never found.
The tinker boys and the sheriff's men
shaking the tallest tree.
And we sat and watched their women hide.
Laughed so much we split our sides.
Scattered horses that they would ride —
mayhem in the high degree.

We crossed through fields of midnight green
often heard but seldom seen.
Tore down hedges, stripping leaves —
no-one could quite agree
whether we came from north or south.
We stole the screams from out their mouths
and go where no man would allow
mayhem in the high degree.

Like scaly carp and feathered swan
to nature's world we do belong.
We ride the thin winds of the night
and set dark spirits free.
We terrified the mare and foal.
The fox stood still and far too bold.
So we strung him up, brush neatly folded —
mayhem, maybe.

Overhang

Good morning, gentlemen. Why the uneasy frowns?
Too much everything, and I can't recall. Did I let you down?
Nobody will answer me. Makes me feel that I want to die.
My mind is inclined to lie.
Oh, no – think I did it last night again.
Oh, no – been out on the overhang again.

My hotel room was a battleground.
How did I find my way?
My wallet's gone and my jacket's torn.
My memory's a hazy grey.
Do I seem to remember now, two creatures about eight feet tall?
No safety net to break my fall.
Oh, no – must have done it last night again.
Oh, no – crawled out on the overhang again.
Been out on the overhang.

Watching demons and spirits glide.
Heading out to the nearest star.
Better lead me back to the bar.
Oh, no – might do it tonight again.
Oh, no – crawl out on the overhang again.
Been out on the overhang.
Crawling out on the overhang.
Out on the overhang.

Kelpie

There was a warm wind with the high tide
on the south side of the hill.
When a young girl went a-walking
and I followed with a will.
»Good day to you, my fine young lady
with your lips so sweetly full.
May I help you comb your long hair –
sweep it from that brow so cool?«

Up, ride with the kelpie[1].
I'll steal your soul to the deep.
If you don't ride with me while the devil's free
I'll ride with somebody else.

Well, I'm a man when I'm feeling
the urge to step ashore.
So I may charm you – not alarm you.
Tell you all fine things, and more.
Up, ride with the kelpie.
I'll steal your soul to the deep.
If you don't ride with me while the devil's free
I'll ride with somebody else.

Say goodbye to all your dear kin –
for they hate to see you go
in your young prime, to this place of mine
in the still loch far below.
Up, ride with the kelpie.
I'll steal your soul to the deep.
If you don't ride with me while the devil's free
I'll ride with somebody else.

1 Kelpie: figure in Celtic mythology; half man, half horse; lives mostly in water

Living In These Hard Times

The bone's in the china. The fat's in the fire.
There's no turkey left on the table.
The commuter's return on the six o'clock flyer
brings no bale of hay for the stable.
Well, the light, it is failing along the green belt
as we follow the hard road signs.
Semi-detached in our suburban-ness –
we're living in these hard times.

Well the fly's in the milk and the cat's in the stew.
Another bun in the oven – oh, what to do?
We'll laugh and we'll sing and try to bring
a pound from your pocket.
Good day to you.
Oh, these hard times.

The politicians sat on the wall
and traded with the union game.
Someone slapped a writ on our deficit –
not a penny left to our name.
Oh, the times are hard and the credits lean,
and they toss and they turn in sleep.
And the line they take is the line they make –
but it's not the line they keep.

The cow jumped over yesterday's moon
and the lock ran away with the key.
You know what you like, and you like what you know
but there is no jam for tea.
Well, the light it is failing along the green belt
as we follow the hard road signs.
Semi-detached in our suburban-ness –
we're living in these hard times.

III. THE ESSENTIAL TULL

Witches Promise (*Living In The Past*)
Bungle In The Jungle (*WarChild*)
Farm On The Freeway (*Crest Of A Knave*)
Thick As A Brick (*Thick As A Brick*)
Sweet Dream (*Living In The Past*)
The Clasp (*The Broadsword And The Beast*)
Pibroch (Pee-Break) / Black Satin Dancer (Instrumental)
Fallen On Hard Times (*The Broadsword And The Beast*)
Cheap Day Return (*Aqualung*)
Wond'ring Aloud (*Aqualung*)
Dun Ringill (*Stormwatch*)
Life's A Long Song (*Living In The Past*)
One White Duck/0^{10} = Nothing At All (*Minstrel In The Gallery*)
Songs From The Wood (*Songs From The Wood*)
Living In The Past (*Living In The Past*)
Teacher (*Living In The Past*)
Aqualung (*Aqualung*)
Locomotive Breath (*Aqualung*)

ROCK ISLAND

September 1989

Kissing Willie
The Rattlesnake Trail
Ears Of Tin
Undressed To Kill
Rock Island
Heavy Water
Another Christmas Song
The Whaler's Dues
Big Riff And Mando
Strange Avenues

Kissing Willie

Breaking hearts in a market town. She eats fillet of sole
and washes it down with sparkling wine.
Nice girl, but a bad girl's better. Qualifies in both ways
to my mind. But now she's kissing Willie.

She shows a leg – shows it damn well. Knows how to drive a man
right back to being a child.
Well, she's a – nice girl, but her bad girl's better. I can read
it in her cheating eyes and know that in a while – well,
she'll be kissing Willie. (My best friend Willie.)

Willie stands and Willie falls. Willie hangs his head
behind grey factory walls.
She's a – nice girl, but her bad girl's better. Me and Willie
just can't help come, when she calls.
Now she's kissing Willie. (My best friend Willie.)

The Rattlesnake Trail

I wear a hair shirt round my shoulder. Got a cold stew in my spoon.
And I'm falling on my head, lifting feet of lead –
now it's got me baying at the moon.
Well, there's a race on for tomorrow. I'm stretching out
for what might have been.
Going to come out from the night, get my second sight –
play rough – you know what I mean.
I'm going for the kill. I'm going tooth and nail
up that dusty hill – on the rattlesnake trail.

Got the law laid down to the left of me. Got the real world to the right.
Heading up through the middle with my cat and my fiddle –
yeah, looking for a fight.
Going to ride hard in bandit country – on the blind side of the bend.
Keep my nose to the wind while the rabbit's skinned –
bed down at the journey's end. (Be a rattlesnake.)
I'm going for the kill. I'm going tooth and nail
up that dusty hill – on the rattlesnake trail.

The rattlesnake trail.
I'm going on the rattlesnake trail.

Going to be with wolves in winter – run in angry packs by day.
But when you give a dog a bone, he has to be alone –
growl, keep the other dogs away.
See that thin moon on the mountain. See that cold star in the sky.
Going to bring them down – shake them to the ground –
put that apple in the pie. (Be a rattlesnake.)
I'm going for the kill. I'm going tooth and nail
up that dusty hill – on the rattlesnake trail.

Ears Of Tin

In the last hours of a sunset rendezvous –
chill breeze against tide, that carries me from you.
Got a job in a southern city – got some lead-free in my tank.
Now I must whisper goodbye – I'm bound for the mainland.

Island in the city. Cut by a cold sea.
People moving on an ocean. Groundswell of humanity.

Now the sun breaks through rain as I climb Glen Shiel[1]
on the trail of those old cattlemen who drove their bargain south again.
And in the eyes of those five sisters of Kintail[2]
there's a wink of seduction from the mainland.

Island in the city. Cut by a cold sea.
People moving on an ocean. Groundswell of humanity.
Storm-lashed on the high-rise – their words are spray to the wind.
Blown like silent laughter. Falling on ears of tin.

Take my heart and take my brawn.
Take by stealth or take by storm –
set my brain to *cruise*.
I can see the glow of suburb lights.
I'm fresh from the out-world –
singing the mainland blues.

There was a girl where I came from.
Seems like a long time, long time gone by.
Wears the west wind in her hair.
She calls from the hill – yeah, she calls
in my mainland blues.

There's a coast road that winds to heaven's door
where a fat ferry floats on muted diesel roar.
And there's a light on the hillside – and there's a flame in her
eyes, but how cold the lights burn on the mainland.

1 Glen Shiel: gorge in the west of Scotland
2 Five Sisters of Kintail: range of mountains, close to Glen Shiel

Island in the city. Cut by a cold sea.
People moving on an ocean. Groundswell of humanity.
Storm-lashed on the high-rise – their words are spray to the wind.
Blown like silent laughter. Falling on ears of tin
in my mainland blues.

Undressed To Kill

Working on the late shift – first drink of the day.
Pull a chair up to the table, have to look the other way.
What kind of place am I in? And who's this over here?
Shaking through the silver bubbles climbing through my beer.
Won't let it move me, but I can't sit still.
Could you meet the eyes of a working girl
undressed to kill.

Staring through the smoke haze – plaid shirts in the night.
Well, I'm making sure that everything is zipped up tight.
Who's that jumping on the table? Putting tonic in my gin?
Brushing silken dollars on her cold white skin.
Won't let it move me, but I can't sit still.
Could you meet the eyes of a working girl
undressed to kill.

She could have been sweet seventeen. There again, well, so could I.
There was a tear drop sparkle on the inside of her thigh.
Going to fetch myself a cold beer. I've got to get a grip.
Find some place to touch down. Find a landing strip.
Won't let it move me, but I can't sit still.
Can you meet the eyes of a working girl
undressed to kill.

Last one out is a cold duck. Paddling down the road.
I wait outside, my motor running – got a warm dream to unload.
Can I face her in the sunshine? In the harsh real light of day?
She walks out with recognition in her eyes – I look away.
Won't let it move me, but I can't sit still.
Couldn't meet the eyes of a working girl
undressed to kill.

Rock Island

Savage night on a misty island. Lights wink out in the
canyon walls.
Two old boys in a stolen racer. Black rubber contrails in
the unwashed halls.
And all roads out of here seem to lead right back to the
Rock Island.

I've gone from here to Paris, London, and even riding on a
jumbo to Bombay.
The long haul back holds faint attraction, but the people
there know they're o.k.
See the girl following the red balloon: walking all alone
on her Rock Island.

Doesn't everyone have their own Rock Island? Their own little
patch of sand?
Where the slow waves crawl and your angels fall and you find
you can hardly stand.
And just as you're drowning, well, the tide goes down.
And you're back on your Rock Island.

Hey there, girlie with the torn dress, shaking: who was it
touched you? Who was it ruined your day?
Whose footprint calling card? And what they want, stepping
on your beach anyway?
I'll be your life raft out of here, but you'd only drift right
back to your Rock Island.

Hey, boy with the personal stereo: nothing 'tween the ears
but that hard rock sound.
Playing to your empty room, empty guitar tune. No use waiting
for that C.B.S. to come around.
'Cos all roads out of here seem to lead right back to your
Rock Island.

Heavy Water

I walked out in the city night.
A burning in my eyes, like it was broad daylight.
And it was hot, down there in the crowd.
The stars went out behind a thunder cloud.
Chatter in the air, like a telegraph line.
Big drops hissing on the neon sign.
Thumping in my heart, and it's hurting me to see.
Smokestack blowing, now they're pouring
heavy water on me.

She was a southern girl. We stared man to man.
I moved like a stranger in this strange land.
She was a round hole, I was a square peg.
I watched the little black specks running down her leg.
Didn't seem to mind that dirty rain coming down –
shirt hanging open. She was wet and brown.
Thumping in my heart, and it's hurting me to see.
Smokestack blowing, now they're pouring
heavy water on me.

What goes up has to fall back down.
It's no night to be out dancing in a party town
when it runs hot and it runs so wide –
running in the street like a thin black tide.
Chatter in the air, like a telegraph line.
Big drops hissing on the neon sign.
Thumping in my heart, and it's hurting me to see.
Smokestack blowing, now they're pouring
heavy water on me.

Another Christmas Song

Hope everybody's ringing on their own bell, this fine morning.
Hope everyone's connected to that long distance phone.
Old man, he's a mountain.
Old man, he's an island.
Old man, he's a-waking says
»I'm going to call, call all my children home.«

Hope everybody's dancing to their own drum this fine morning –
the beat of distant Africa or a Polish factory town.
Old man, he's calling for his supper.
Calling for his whisky.
Calling for his sons and daughters, yeah –
calling all his children round.

Sharp ears are tuned in to the drones and chanters warming.
Mist blowing round some headland, somewhere in your memory.
Everyone is from somewhere –
even if you've never been there.
So take a minute to remember the part of you
that might be the old man calling me.

How many wars you're fighting out there, this winter's morning?
Maybe it's always time for another Christmas song.
Old man he's asleep now.
Got appointments to keep now.
Dreaming of his sons and daughters, and proving –
proving that the blood is strong.

The Whaler's Dues

Money speaks. Soft hearts lose. The truth only whispers.
It's the whaler's dues.

I've been running on diesel. Been running on coal.
Running on borrowed time, if truth's to be told.
Two whales in the ocean, cruising the night
search for each other before we turn out their light.

Been accused of deep murder on the North Atlantic swell
but I have three hungry children and a young wife as well.
And behind stand generations of hard hunting men
who raised a glass to the living, and went killing again.
Are you with me?

Money speaks. Soft hearts lose. The truth only whispers.
Now pay the whaler's dues.
Can you forgive me?

Now I'm old and I sit land-locked in a back-country jail
to reflect on all of my sins and the death of the whale.
Send me back down the ages. Put me to sea once again
when the oceans were full – yes, and men would be men.
Can you forgive me?

Big Riff And Mando

Marty loved the sound of the stolen mandolin.
Somebody took it on a dare in the night-time.
Ran up to the radio, calling out to the wind.
Now, bring it, bring it back at least an hour before flight time.
It was a souvenir, but it was a right arm missing.
Swap a woodwork rhythm for a humbucking[1] top line.

Big Riff, rough boy, wants to be a singer in a band.
A little slow in the brain box, but he had a quick right hand.
Run left, run right – everywhere he look –
nobody watching, no, but that was
all he took last night.

Running on the power of a stolen mandolin.
Steal a little inspiration. Steal a little muscle.
Will he wake in the morning, wondering – was it really worth it?
So make a little deal. Yeah, make a little hustle.

Ringing on the radio – got a proposition for those English boys.
I'll make the sing-song – you can make the background noise.
One, two, three, four – one bar and in.
Give you back the mando, if you let this singer sing tonight.

Marty loved the sound of the stolen mandolin.
Big Riff took it on a dare in the night-time.
Now it's four o'clock, and we're waiting at the sound-check.
Looking for a face staring in from the sunshine.
We got two strong lawmen from the sheriff's office.
They're going to lift Big Riff before he plays the first line.

Big Riff, rough boy, wants to be a singer in a band.
Yeah, help him on the stage now, put that microphone in his hand.
Think hard, think right – nothing in his mind –
so Riff did a runner, but he left the mandolin behind.

1 Humbucker: special type of pick-up for guitars

Strange Avenues

Strange avenues where you lose all sense of direction
and everywhere is Main Street in the winter sun.
The wino sleeps – cold coat lined with the money section.
Looking like a record cover from 1971.

And here am I – warm feet and a limo waiting.
Shall I make us both feel good? And would a dollar do?
But in your streets, I have no credit rating
and it might not take a lot to be alone just like you.

Heading up and out now, from your rock island.
Really good to have had you here with me.
And somewhere in the crowd I think I hear a young girl whisper
»Are you ever lonely, just like me?«

CATFISH RISING

September 1991

This Is Not Love
Occasional Demons
Roll Yer Own
Rocks On The Road
Sparrow On The Schoolyard Wall
Thinking Round Corners
Still Loving You Tonight
Doctor To My Disease
Like A Tall Thin Girl
White Innocence
Sleeping With The Dog
Gold-Tipped Boots, Black Jacket And Tie
When Jesus Came To Play
Night In The Wilderness

This Is Not Love

Winds howled. Rains spit down.
All these nights playing precious games.
Cheap hotel in some seaboard town
closed down for the winter and whispered names.
Puppy-dog waves on a big moon sea
snap our heels half-heartedly
and how come you know better than me
that this is not love.
No, this is not love.

Empty drugstore postcards freeze
sunburst images of summers gone.
Think I see us in these promenade days
before we learned October's song.
Out on the headland, one gale-whipped tree;
curious, head bent to see.
And how come you know better than me
that this is not love.

Down to the sad south, smokey plumes
mark that real world city home.
Broken spells and silent gloom
ooze from that concrete honeycomb.
Puppy-dog waves on a big moon sea
snapped our heels half-heartedly
and how come you know better than me
that this is not love.

Occasional Demons

Well, you got a big-jib crane waiting to pick you up.
Mmmm, you see those snakes that crawl, they're just dying
to trip you up.
Live out in sad shacks at the back of town.
Hold your breath while we do you down
'cos we're all kinds of animals coming here:
occasional demons too.

Well, you got a nice apartment here with appliances and CD.
We're gonna leave your stereo, but we'll have your soul for tea.
I'm not speaking of material things.
Gonna chew you up, gonna suck you in
'cos we're all kinds of animals coming here:
occasional demons too.

Smokestacks, belching black, we're the have-nots in your shade.
How about a slice of life, how about some
human trade?
Eat at the best table in town.
No headwaiter going to turn us down
'cos we're all kinds of animals coming here:
occasional demons too.

Roll Yer Own

Roll yer own. Don't mean you got no money.
Only that you got no opportunity to shake it with that friend of mine.
Roll yer own if you can't buy readymade;
if you won't be satisfied when you feel the sudden need
to unwind.
You know what moves you in the wee hours
when there's nothing on the answerphone.
And if you don't get enough of that electric love
don't try to get by –
roll yer own, roll it when there's no-one listening:
when those re-runs play on the late-night
black and white TV.
Roll yer own, roll it when there's something missing
and those wild cats howl, running in the moonshine.

Roll yer own: you got to hit that spot.
Roll yer own when your hands are hot.

Rocks On The Road

There's a black cat down on the quayside.
Ship's lights, green eyes glowing in the dark.
Two young cops handing out a beating:
know how to hurt and leave no mark.
Down in the half-lit bar of the hotel
there's a call for the last round of the day.
Push back the stool, take that elevator ride.
Fall in bed and kick my shoes away.
Rocks on the road.

Can't sleep through the wild sound of the city.
Hear a car full of young boys heading for a fight.
Long distance telephone keeps ringing out engaged:
wonder who you're talking with tonight.
Who you talking with tonight?
Rocks on the road.

Tired plumbing wakes me in the morning.
Shower runs hot, runs cold playing with me.
Well, I'm up for the down side, life's a bitch
and all that stuff:
so come and shake some apples from my tree.
Have to pay for my minibar madness.
Itemised phone bill overload.
Well now, how about some heavy rolling?
Move these rocks on the road.

Crumbs on the breakfast table.
And a million other little things to spoil my day.
Now how about a little light music
to chase it all away?
To chase it all away.

Sparrow On The Schoolyard Wall

You want to be a bookworm? You wanna be aloof?
You wanna sit in judgement, looking down from the roof?
Try a wee sensation: but first you have to want to join in.
You should be, should be raging down the freeway
with some friends from the mall.
Don't stay forever in your limbo: fly before you fall
little sparrow on the schoolyard wall.

So dress a little dangerous and modify your walk.
There's nothing wrong with sparrows, but try
to be a sparrowhawk.
Hunting in the evening and floating in the heat in the day.
You might, might acquire some predatory instinct.
Do the wolf pack crawl.
Don't stay forever in your limbo: fly before you fall
little sparrow on the schoolyard wall.

Well, I don't want to be your daddy.
Don't want to be your engineer of sin.
And I don't want to play the piper here.
I'm only banging on a mandolin
and anyway, you're just a little sparrow
on the schoolyard wall.

There's nothing wrong with learning. Nothing wrong
with your books.
So exercise some judgement. Too much broth can spoil the cook.
Feel a little sensation and know when it's time to join in.
You should be, should be raging down the freeway
with some friends from the mall.
Don't stay forever in your limbo: fly before you fall
little sparrow on the schoolyard wall.

Thinking Round Corners

All of you sit up in bed. Don't think in straight lines ahead.
Can't sleep? Head spin? Don't think in circles, it'll do you in.
Think back to the dream you had; no sense of being good or bad.
Jump to the left, jump to the right. Think round corners into night.

Let's go in wet corridors: dive down drains.
Draw strength from machinery, it's all the same.
Thinking round corners. Think round corners, I say.

Pretty girl with neon eyes: best man between white thighs.
Bridegroom didn't know a thing: got his love in lights,
she wears two rings.
Think back to that dream you had.
Blue boy sorry, pink girl sad.
Yellow cow, big-eyed moon all coming round the corner soon.

Let's stand in rapids: cling to carnivals.
Spit life from the maypole in savage ceremony.
Let's go in wet corridors: dive down drains.
Draw strength from machinery, it's all the same.
Thinking round corners. Think round corners, I say.

Paper cowboys, tin drums banging where the white man comes.
Landowners with whips and chains but soft in bed amidst
warm rains.
Thinking back to the dream they had. Jack and Jill.
Jack the lad.
Homestead. Home free. How about leaving some for me?

Let's bathe in malt whisky: covet gold finery
through the eyes of a Jackdaw, dressed to the nines.
Let's go in wet corridors: dive down drains.
Draw strength from machinery, it's all the same.
Thinking round corners. Think round corners, I say.
Thinking round corners.

Still Loving You Tonight

It's a lonely life I live and I live this life to go
and if I leave you with one thing it's just that I want
you to know
I'll still be loving you tonight.
I left flowers on your table, left the lock on your door.
Staked a claim in your heartlands, put grain in your store.
I'll still be loving you tonight.

Got fingers on the button of that telephone dial.
Call in and move your mountains, fill your spaces while
I'm still loving you tonight.

You want to know how I can leave you?
How can I move along this way?
Too much of a good thing can make you crazy
and it's a good thing that happened to me today.
I'll still be loving you tonight.

Doctor To My Disease

I've been treated for mild depression
and I've been treated for growing pains.
I've been treated for hallucinations;
now I can see it all coming again.
Well, you can wind me up. Yeah, you can slow me down.
You can dig a little, and you can mess me around.
But there's one thing I should tell you, to which
you must agree:
There's no use you playing doctor to my disease.
Said it's no use you playing doctor to my disease.

I got no cure for this condition
that you've been causing me tonight.
Well, you put my heart in overdrive:
hand me the bullet I must bite.
You can stir me up and you can cut me down.
You can probe a little, push that knife around.
But there's one thing I should tell you, to which
you must agree:
It's no use you playing doctor to my disease.

Do you have to break my engine
so you can fix it up again?
Tuned to crazy imperfection
just to score me out of ten.
Well, you can wind me up. Yeah, you can slow me down.
You can dig a little. Yeah, you can mess me around.
But there's one thing I should tell you, to which
you must agree:
That it's no use you playing doctor to my disease.

Like A Tall Thin Girl

Well, I don't care to eat out in smart restaurants.
I'd rather do a Vindaloo[1]: take away is what I want.
I was down at the old Bengal, having telephoned a treat
when I saw her framed in the kitchen door.
She looked good enough to eat.
(And I mean eat.)
She was a tall thin girl.
She looked like a tall thin girl.
She said, »Whose is this carry-out?«
My face turned chilli red.
Well, I don't know about carrying out,
but you can carry me off to bed.
(And I mean bed.)
She was a tall thin girl.
She moved like a tall thin girl.
Maybe I can fetch for it,
and maybe I can stretch for it.

I may not be a fat man and I'm not exactly small
but when it all comes down, couldn't stand my ground.
This girl was tall.
(And I mean tall.)

Big boy Doane[2], he's a drummer. Don't play no tambourine
but he's Madras[1] hot on the bongo trot,
if you know just what I mean.
Stands six foot three in his underwear;
going to get him down here and see
if this good lady's got a little sister 'bout the same size as me.
She was a tall thin girl.
She looked like a tall thin girl.
Well, can I fetch for it?
Well, maybe I can stretch for it?
Well, am I up for it? Or do I have to go down for it?

1 Vindaloo and Madras: Indian dishes
2 Big boy Doane: Doane Perry; drummer with Jethro Tull in the *Catfish Rising* period

White Innocence

She drifted from some minor festival.
Didn't look like any summer of love:
just a thousand weekend warriors in a muddy field.
She was the hand to fit my glove.
Funny thing, the innocence of the lonely.
Funny thing, the charm of the young.

See how she moves just like two angels (in white innocence).
Yet one of them is on the run.
The other's tapping at my car window
and I'm squinting through the sun
trying to see if she's some child of the nineties:
or just another dangerous fantasy of mine.
Yeah. White innocence.
She was white innocence.

A perfect hole was in her stocking:
it made a perfect window to her heart.
I could have moved among her waterfalls:
her misty curtains drawn apart.
Did she see warm safety in my numbers
to want to hitch a ride this way?
Felt like I was taking her to market now
to be sold as the last lot of the day.
Funny thing, the distance of the lonely.
Funny thing, the charm of the young.
White innocence.

She pressed the button, lowered the window:
let her hand trail in the slipstream of the night.
A frost from nowhere seemed to lick her fingers:
I could have warmed them, but the moment wasn't right.
Obvious, she was headed nowhere special:
yes, well it was even obvious to me.
I was doing some, some watching, some waiting:
she'd been here before, most definitely.

There was the promise of early bed-time.
There was the promise of heaven on earth.
Think I was sending out low-voltage electricity:
played it right down for what it was worth.
She turned and looked at me in white innocence
and with the clearest eyes of forever grey
she rested one small hand for a second on my knee:
I stopped the car. She walked away.
Funny thing, the wisdom of the lonely.
Funny thing, the charm of the young.
Away you go now.
White innocence.

Sleeping With The Dog

Her love is like a candle: you light it up at night.
Her heart is like a pack of cards: one chance to guess it right.
Sometimes I do.
She's got a tongue like a viper, but she can whisper like a dove.
Soft touch like brushed velvet: till she hits you from above.
And sometimes she does.

She leaves me breathing: down like a fallen log.
Just when I feel like dancing
I wake up sleeping with the dog.
And it goes: (woof) sleeping with the dog.

I have to guess at the mysteries of her unfathomable soul.
Guess when the time seems right
to make a broken spirit whole
and that time is due. C'm'on.

She leaves me breathing: down like a fallen log
and just when I feel like dancing
I wake up sleeping with the dog.
And it goes: (woof) sleeping with the dog.

Gold-Tipped Boots, Black Jacket And Tie

I'm battered and bruised. I got lines I can't use.
My head won't deliver. Well, I'm sold down the river.
But I'm turning again.
Yes, 'n' I'm turning again.
Well, I'm turning again.
And I'm turning again.
Wearing gold-tipped boots, black jacket and tie.

Well, I've been second to none:
this horse was ready to run.
Now I'm has-been and used:
disarmed and de-fused
but I'm turning again.
And I'm turning again.
Yes, 'n' I'm turning again.
I'm turning again.
Wearing gold-tipped boots, black jacket and tie.

I'm egg over-easy
and I'm washing-up squeezy.
Appliance for sale:
fat wind in my sail
and I'm turning again.
Yes, 'n' I'm turning again.
Well, I'm turning again.
Yes, 'n' I'm turning again.
Wearing gold-tipped boots, black jacket and tie.
Well, I'm turning again.

When Jesus Came To Play

I was in my watering-hole with some ugly friends of mine
when the door came off its hinges like a cork from fizzy wine.
He said, »My name is Jesus: I'm the leader of the band.
Got to set up my equipment, if you boys can lend a hand.«
Oh yeah. When Jesus came to play.

He set that bandstand jumping. Yeah, and he cranked it up so loud.
And he moved up to the microphone: had the attention of the crowd.
He said, »My name is Jesus: going to turn your head around.
I'm going to make this easy. Got no time to mess around.«
Oh yeah. When Jesus came to play.

»I got no twelve disciples, and I got no cross to bear.
If you thought they had me crucified, I guess you weren't there.«
Oh yeah. When Jesus came to play. When Jesus came …

He sang about three or four numbers, but we'd heard it all before.
We boys were getting restless: no girls were moving on the floor.
Those parables, they were merciless and the tables overturned.
And there were no minor miracles
but false prophets they were burned.
Well, maybe he was Jesus;
but his hair could have used a comb.
Long before he hit the last notes, we boys had all gone home.
Oh yeah. When Jesus came to play.

Oh Jesus, is it really you?

Night In The Wilderness

I could be sitting on the left of you.
You'd be looking straight ahead.
If I was adrift right across from you,
you still would cut me dead.
I've had better deep discussions
with this plate of soft-shelled crab.

I'd put some spice in your rice.
You'd give me blues in the stew.
I'd give you catfish jumping.
You'd give me all this work to do.
Who's got the cheque on this hot dinner?
Who's got the tabs on the crab?

Another night in the wilderness:
should have been a night on the town.
Lesson in learning: how to hold a conversation down.
I'm in splendid isolation, feel that heavy silence fall.
Got all this cut out for me to do.
Another night in the wilderness of you.

Here I am drinking you with my eyes.
You're looking at the gravy on my bib.
I go weak-kneed at the suggestion of you.
What's wrong with the cut of my jib?
Is there a lobster in the offing, or just a fifty dollar cheque?

Captions

Photo Credits

Song Index

290

Also available from Palmyra Publishers

Georg Stein

Bob Dylan – Temples In Flames

94 pages · 70 colour and black and white photos
Hardcover · £ 13.95 · ISBN 3-9802298-0-7

*The book includes unique photos of
Dylan's European tour in 1987*

Distributed by:
International Music Publications (IMP)
Southend Road, Woodford Green
Essex IG8 8HN, England
Tel. 081 / 5516131